MW00698823

My Daily Life

My Daily Life

BY
ANTHONY J. PAONE, S.J.

1970

Msgr. Austin P. Bennett, JCD, P.A.
Director of the

CONFRATERNITY OF THE PRECIOUS BLOOD
5300 Ft. Hamilton Pkway, Brooklyn, N.Y. 11219

302

NIHIL OBSTAT:

      MARTINUS S. RUSHFORD, Ph. D.
      Censor Librorum

IMPRIMATUR:

      ✠ FRANCISCUS IOANNES MUGAVERO, D.D
      Episcopus Bruklyniensis

Bruklyni,
Die VIII Aprilis 1970

The Nihil Obstat and Imprimatur are official declarations
that a book or pamphlet is free of doctrinal and moral error.
No implication is contained therein that those who have
granted the Nihil Obstat and Imprimatur agree with the
contents, opinions or statements expressed.

© 1970. Confraternity of the Precious Blood
Printed and bound in the U. S. A.

All Rights Reserved under International Copyright Union.
All Rights Reserved under Pan-American Copyright Convention.

A Personal Message from the Author

Dear Reader,

MOST people achieve some measure of fulfillment and satisfaction in daily life. They also have to cope with some degree of frustration and disappointment in their daily routine. Earthly living is certainly no paradise, but neither is it an utter hell. In one sense, life is what we make it, and in another sense, we are what we permit life to make us. Though we cannot choose all the things we would like to have in this world, we can learn to get some enjoyment and satisfaction from the things that lie within our reach. Thus, every man has a choice of surrendering to his disappointments and wallowing in self-pity, or beginning each new day with renewed attitudes and making the most of his daily circumstances and situations.

FAME, fortune, and success mean different things to different people. What they mean to each one depends on the needs, wants, preferences and prejudices which developed through his past experience, and continue to motivate him today. These appetites and emotions influence his feelings, thinking and decisions more often than he realizes. Even when his intentions are good and his efforts are sincere, he can be mistaken or misguided by these inner forces. Each man has a choice of remaining fixed in his present mental, emotional and spiritual deficiencies, or of growing each day a little more fully into the kind of person he could yet become. Many will deny it, but most people would make some changes in themselves or in their personal life, if they could relive it with the wisdom they have learned from past experience. Though no man can change himself completely, every man can, with good will and reasonable expectations, achieve an appreciable progress in his desired self-renewal.

THE WORD "renewal" became extremely popular throughout the world during the years of the second Vatican Council. Everything said and done before, during and after the council, was presented to the world in the light and spirit of renewal. This renewal was intended to create in each individual a broader, more inspiring vision of his own everyday living. Through this vision, each person was to develop new attitudes toward God, himself, and others. It was to make him more aware of 1) his personal *commitment* to Christ's cause on earth, 2) the *unity* among all men as children of God, and 3) his duty to be a *witness* of Christ by his daily fidelity to Christian faith and principles.

TO SOME people, this kind of renewal sounds like too many changes, too many obstacles, and too much work. They feel that they are not "that religious." To them, being religious means being outstanding, as the cannonized saints were. Others feel that their daily burden of personal obligations and occupations is already heavy enough, without their assuming additional burdens. These people have the idea that God and the Church may burden them beyond their present strength or resources. This is not so. God and the Church simply ask that each person consider how he may enrich his daily routine within the boundaries of his personal talents, gifts, and possibilities. As the custodian of Christian faith and morality, the Church also expects each individual to achieve enough knowledge and training to form his own conscience in time of doubt or indecision. With this inner development, the man of good will can decide for himself, when he can or cannot extend himself beyond his present commitments. This book deals, in large part, with the human misunderstandings and natural obstacles which make this kind of self-renewal more difficult than it has to be.

D O NOT expect to read this book as you might read most other books. It is designed to give more than mere information. It offers the reader a broader understanding and deeper appreciation of human nature as it operates within him and in those with whom he must deal. It is calculated to enlarge the reader's view of human behavior and strengthen his ability to deal more realistically with others. This book tries to help the reader get the most out of daily life. It is a guide to greater peace of mind and increased spiritual vitality. Its ultimate goal is "a more satisfying self-possession and a more enlightened self-management throughout this earthly life." To absorb its message into your very being, will require time, reflection, application, and persevering practice. The paragraphs are numbered to help the reader return to a profitable insight, or to recall its place more easily. In view of this, we would recommend the advice of Francis Bacon: "Read not to contradict and confute, nor to believe and take for granted, nor to find talk and discourse; but to weigh and consider. Some books are to be tasted, others to be swallowed, and some few to be chewed and digested. That is, some books are to be read only in parts, others to be read, but not curiously, and some few to be read wholly, and with diligence and attention." For this volume, we would recommend the last method of reading.

Sincerely,

Anthony J. Paone, S. J.

Contents

PART ONE

Some Reflections on Daily Human Living

IT IS a rare man who has not at one time or another wanted to improve himself in some particular elements that marred his life-style, i.e., his personal manner of facing life and responding to its various situations. Since the second Vatican Council, Christians have been made more aware than ever of the advantages and need to renew one's own spiritual strivings for a greater possession of his inner thinking and his responses to life's daily circumstances. How adult one is, regardless of age and experience, depends on his degree of self-possession and self-management when daily life presents its demands, problems, and conflicts. This section presents an over-all view of the basic requirements for a successful daily growth toward a more self-satisfying fulfillment.

1. Man's Earthly Life
2. Man's Need of Order
3. Human Nature's Resistance to Change
4. Perspective in Daily Life
5. An Invitation to Self-Realization
6. An Effort toward Self-Renewal
7. Self-Understanding in the Effort

I

Man's Earthly Life

IN ONE WAY or another along life's daily
path, every man encounters some experiences which make him aware of his capabilities and limitations, his fulfillment and
frustrations. Being human means having a
nature which is united in some ways and divided in other ways. Of all the living creatures
on earth, man alone can be both for himself
and against himself at the same time. St. Paul
gives a good description of this human situation in his letter to the Romans. He writes:
"I cannot understand my own behavior. I
fail to carry out the things I want to do, and I
find myself doing the very thing I hate . . .
for though to do what is good is in me, the
performance is not, with the result that instead of doing the good thing I want to do, I
carry out the sinful things I do not want . . .
In fact this seems to be the rule, that every
single time I want to do good, it is something
evil that comes to hand. In my inmost self I
dearly love God's law, but I can see that my
body follows a different law that battles the
law which my reason dictates . . . In short, it
is I who with my reason serve the law of God,

and no less I who serve in my unspiritual self
the law of sin.'' (Romans 7: 15-25)

2 In these words St. Paul describes how
man is both divided and integrated within
himself. He is divided because his intelligent
desires are often opposed by his unreasoning
drives, urges, feelings, and emotions. He is
integrated in so far as he constantly seeks his
own well-being. When man acts against his
better judgment, he is reaching out for what
appears desirable at the time. At the same
time, however, his reason may be troubling
him with a sense of danger or an awareness
of guilt.

3 In varying degrees, this inner division of
human nature is experienced by every human
being on earth. It is indeed a rare man who
does not occasionally find himself torn between his unreasoning wants, feelings, and
emotions on the one hand, and his intelligent
desires, ideals, and judgments on the other.
Within the limits of average human experience, this inner conflict is normal to human
nature. In itself it is not a cause for shame
or blame.

4 Since your fellow-man is subject to the
same inner conflict, you will sometimes find
him difficult to understand or impossible to

satisfy. In his efforts to achieve peace within himself, he may expect you to adjust to his emotional needs more than you can at the moment. The resulting interpersonal friction, be it ever so subtle, is apt to disturb you in some degree. In spite of your good will, you may adopt unwise solutions in such situations. You may try to comply with the needs or wishes of others without due regard for your own legitimate needs, limits or obligations, or you may build up unwarranted resentments toward those who merely seem to have no concern for your well-being; or finally, you may feel obliged to withdraw indiscriminately from others, and thereby lose contact with good people who might have been your friends. While each of these solutions may help when wisely applied in individual situations, they are always harmful to you when used as a general solution to all disturbing interpersonal relations.

5   Finally, this inner conflict of your human nature can cause a psychological barrier between you and God. Due to past experience, your unreasoning emotions may cast your self-image in an unfavorable light. You may see yourself as falling short of what you feel you "should be." Moreover, you may sin-

cerely feel that God thinks the same about you. On the other hand, your self-disgust may make you overly sensitive to any reminders of your real or imagined faults. In either case, your image of God will be somewhat frightening or irritating, if not downright repulsive. To make matters more difficult, the above process can occur within your mind without your awareness. Consciously, you may feel no more than some vague uneasiness in religious situations, or simply an unaccountable lack of thought, interest, or spontaneity in formal religious exercises.

6   Since this inner conflict is natural to man, it is inescapable. Every man born into this world, bears his share of it. Sometimes consciously, sometimes semiconsciously, and sometimes unconsciously, every man tries to counterbalance the disrupting effects of his conflicting needs, wants, and established habits. Though there is no perfect solution to this conflict here on earth, it is possible to diminish the emotional pressures, mental uncertainties, and moral deficiencies stemming from it.

7   A number of people seem unable, unwilling, or seriously doubtful about helping themselves in this matter. They daily attend to

most of their other needs, but in this matter of achieving peace of mind, harmony with others, and a more satisfying religious performance, they feel a certain hopelessness. Many would like a simple solution, quick results, or a perfect achievement. The thought of a planned effort over a period of time, to achieve a gradual progression toward a limited improvement, is too much for them. Consequently, they live each day dominated by the same ignorance, defects, and faults from one end of the year to the next.

8 Jesus came to earth to lead man toward his best possible self-fulfillment both here and hereafter. He does not look on this earthly life as unimportant. He does not expect you to despise the good things of this earthly life. He wants you to seek your intelligent self-fulfillment by making the most of your natural talents, opportunities, and circumstances. He does, however, urge you to look on this earthly life as your path to a fuller life with Him in heaven. Even a professed atheist sees the need of preferring some things to others for his own welfare. He tries to control his unreasoning feelings when he sees them as obstacles to his well-being. Would you be less reasonable in your daily life?

9 Though your intelligence and faith may agree with the above, you may still have misgivings about your ability to give a satisfactory religious performance in your daily life. You may need to reflect often on the truth that "God is reasonable. He will not burden you beyond your strength, nor test you beyond your endurance." Having made your human nature, God knows only too well that it will still make itself felt, in spite of all the supernatural gifts He has bestowed on you. Under the stress of your natural wants, emotional needs, and spontaneous doubts, your faith in Him will waiver at times. There will be days when you will feel utterly alone, unimportant, and even worthless. You may feel as though God is far away from you, or that He does not care about you, or even that He does not exist. You may be strongly inclined to believe your "feelings" rather than your "faith." At such times you may have a deeper appreciation of the sentiments of Jesus Crucified when He cried out, "My God, my God, why have you deserted me?" (Matt. 27:46) If you cannot cling to God in His glory on those days, you can surely cling to Jesus Who underwent the same human experience for your sake.

10   You may feel too weak, too selfish, or even too unworthy to presume that you can compare your "puny" misery to the indescribable misery of Christ Crucified. If so, you need to understand Jesus more fully. He embraced your human nature, in order to share with you your human experience. By so doing, He intended to show you the boundless love of God more convincingly. As He put it to His apostle, "To have seen me is to have seen the Father." (John 14:9) In other words, Jesus, the Image of His Father, showed us the Father in His own personality and example.

11   Even though you may not doubt God because of Himself, you can still have doubts about your own worthiness. Once again you need to understand Christ's message to you. God loves you not so much because of what you have done in your life, but because of what He has done in your life. He made you to His own image and likeness. In all God's earthly creation, man is His most perfect image. Though you may have sinned many times over, the main burden of your redemption lies not upon your shoulders, but on the shoulders of God's divine son, Jesus. From Conception to Crucifixion, Jesus lived His human existence as an act of love and re-

demption for you personally. He has paid the
price of your sins. He instituted sacraments
to raise you to a supernatural state of life
even in this world, and to restore you to that
state as often as you might fall from it by sin.
By developing a positive attitude of good will
in your daily routine, you are cooperating
with your Redeemer in fulfilling God's divine
plan for the world.

12   Do not expect to feel all this. It is not a
matter of "feeling." It is a matter of "fact"
on God's part, and a matter of "faith" on
your part. Jesus Himself often experienced
the commonplace human "feelings" that you
experience in your everyday living. He did
not allow His divinity to give Him any "extraordinary" assistance in these experiences.
As a man, He was like us in all things, except
sin. (Hebrews 4:15) Thus, His human feelings didn't "like" a number of situations and
circumstances, just as your human feelings
dislike certain things in your daily life.

13   Your life today and every day until you
leave this world, is a human experience.
Therefore, you will find yourself divided
against yourself at times, against your neighbor sometimes, and perhaps even divided by
doubts, fears, or rebellion against God some-

times. On the other hand, you will also have your periods of inner peace, external harmony and a satisfying measure of self-possession. During these periods, you will experience a more balanced outlook on life and exercise more positive attitudes in your moments of mental indecision and emotional stress. You will be more disposed to counterbalance your negative emotions and unreasonable tendencies with a more realistic philosophy of life and a firmer faith in God's fatherly involvement in everything that concerns your true well-being.

14 With this larger view of life, you will find your daily experience less disappointing, less frightening, and less aggravating. With a realistic respect for your natural abilities and a prudent estimate of your daily difficulties, problems, and frustrations, you will accept the challenge of everyday living, without straining beyond your powers nor settling for less than you can achieve. God will work with you in your efforts. He will not turn away from you in your moments of weakness or failure. He did not create you to lose you, but to assist you daily toward the eternal fulfillment for which your spirit yearns. With Him you cannot fail, no matter how few your

talents, how weak your good will, and how
poor your daily performance.

2

Man's Need of Order

¹A NUMBER of people look on God as an
intruder in their personal lives. They
feel that He places impossible obligations and
unreasonable restrictions on them. They consider daily life hard enough, without having
to worry about God's super-imposed rules
and regulations. These people are mistaken.
Their notion of God and His commandments
is far from the truth. God did not create man
to carry burdens beyond his strength. Neither
does He desire to test man's virtue or prove
his sincerity by sending him needless disappointments, useless frustrations, or arbitrary
commands. Your ordinary daily life has its
own natural disappointments and frustrations.
Your human nature has its built-in laws.
These laws require you to observe a certain
order. They put definite limits on what you
can do safely, and indicate what constitutes
a threat to your health of body, peace of
mind, and moral self-possession. For ex-

ample, if you overeat, you must be prepared
to suffer some discomfort or worse. No need
to feel that God is punishing you. He simply
lets nature take its course.

2   God would have every man strive for his
earthly fulfillment in every legitimate way
open to him. On the other hand, God also
expects man to seek his fulfillment within
the bounds of reason and reality. Having
endowed man with intelligence, God expects
man to direct his daily conduct with due
regard for the nature and purpose of the
things at his disposal. The man who refuses
to use his powers of reason and conduct
himself with an intelligent self-management,
must be prepared to suffer the natural consequences of his disorderly conduct. An animal
cannot help acting on its feelings, but man
has the spiritual power to evaluate his feelings and judge, with varying degrees of ac-
curacy, whether his feelings are reasonable or
not. True, man is sometimes mentally confused and morally weakened by his inner
needs and conflicts, because his emotions
and feelings influence his thinking and decisions more than usual at such times. God
knows how to take such occasions into consideration. He merely expects each man to

manage himself as wisely and freely as he is able at any given time.

3 God does not expect you to be anxious or over-cautious about your daily activities and occupations. You do not have to think constantly about your every feeling, thought, desire, word or action, to determine whether your behavior is correct or pleasing to God. You simply need to adopt an attitude of good will and a general intention to live your daily life as intelligently and reasonably as you can, with God's help. As for God's help, you may be sure that He will not deny whatever assistance you may need at any moment. Not every misbehavior of yours is due to bad will on your part. It can proceed from inadvertence, ignorance, or even moral weakness at the moment.

4 God speaks to man through nature as well as through His supernatural grace. You cannot disregard the laws of nature without creating some kind of disorder either in yourself, in others, or in the things around you. Nature thrives on balance and order. All of the sciences devised by man, are based upon man's perception of the balance and order required by the various natural forces in his universe. The more man understands and

appreciates the forces of nature, so much the more can he make a wise use of the natural resources at his disposal. So too, as you consider the commandments of God, you will find them based on the nature of man and the nature of daily earthly living. They are not, for the most part, an extra set of rules, added to the laws already governing your human nature.

5 Reflect often on the wisdom of giving due consideration to your human nature, and to the nature of the people and things involved in your daily life. Do not be surprised when you find it hard to understand yourself, with your conflicting needs and wants. The brute beast finds life much simpler, because he is controlled by his feelings and emotions. Man, on the other hand, can learn to understand, utilize, arrange, and improve the things at his disposal. He can enrich not only his personal life, but also the world around him.

6 You may feel that your life is much too small or unimportant to deserve much appreciation or respect. Your attitude toward yourself may be your biggest obstacle to your mental, emotional, and spiritual development. And yet, basic human nature is God's greatest creation in this world. Little as you may see

in yourself worthy of admiration, you are a reflection of the spiritual nature of God. This is an objective fact. It does not depend on your achievements, limitations or failures. This personal worth was bestowed on you by God's own creative hand.

7 The wise man tries to see himself as he is, with his God-given personal nature, his personal endowments, be they many or few, great or small. He is like the servant in the Gospel, who received less than the first servant, and more than the third. He goes forth with respect for the limited talents he has received, and increases their worth by an intelligent use of them. Jesus said that the second servant was praised as highly by his master as the more gifted one. If you could see God in this light, you would have a greater respect for yourself, you would find it easier to "be glad that you are you." With this attitude, you would find yourself more disposed to improve what you can in your daily life, without feeling deprived or frustrated by the real limitations of your nature or station in life.

8 Things are to be valued not for their bigness or littleness, but for their ability to perform the task for which they were made.

A tiny screw in a precious watch is less admired than its jewels and precious metals. And yet the running of the watch may depend more on the screw than on the jewels or metals. God loves the man who knows how to value his achievement in life, and sees it as his participation in God's total work of creation. Such a man is at peace with himself and others because he is content with his portion of reality and his opportunity to make that portion useful.

9 Some people live so much on their negative feelings and emotions that they have no patience with any effort toward "thinking things through." Even when they do profess and sincerely try, to think objectively, their thinking is swayed by their emotional attitudes. Their questions and objections are aimed more at proving what they "feel subjectively" than at seeing how things really are in themselves. Whether maliciously or innocently, they end up believing what they were inclined to believe from the start. Some of these people have a low threshold of pain, stress or frustration. The lower the threshold, the more they feel compelled to liberate themselves from the pressures of mental indecision, emotional conflict, and bodily ten-

sion. Their problem is how to achieve this liberation realistically, i.e., in accordance with the possibilities within their reach.

10 The better you understand the nature of man and his world, the better will you also understand the message of Jesus. Jesus was understanding and sympathetic to those who came to Him. He preached that the truth would make man free. On the other hand He also warned His hearers against an unrealistic liberation. They were not to invent the truth, but to discover it. In His personal life, example, and teaching, He presented a lesson so broad, so profound, so exalted, that a lifetime is not enough to understand it fully.

11 Whatever your limitations, defects, and faults, if you try to base your life on the principle of growth, you will never find life hopelessly dull. Let some little time be set aside each day for reading, reflecting, and conversation with God, so that the passing weeks, months, and years may bring you a healthy growth in your understanding, appreciation and acceptance of the nature you possess and the nature of the people and things involved in your daily life.

3
Human Nature's Resistance to Change

1 YOUR daily life can be dominated by your blind feelings and emotions, or it can be guided by your natural reason and God's supernatural grace. Your feelings and emotions often tend to disregard unpleasant facts, or to doubt those realities which are not visible and tangible. God's grace will add new light to your powers of reason and greater strength to your efforts at self-determination. However, God will not allow His grace to shut off altogether the influence of your natural needs and wants. You will still feel some measure of division within yourself, in spite of your best intentions and sincerest efforts toward a stronger self-possession and a firmer self-management in daily life.

2 The task of reorganizing your thinking and redirecting your external conduct presents a real challenge to you. Your human nature will still tend to fulfill itself through your former attitudes and outlook, your old preferences and prejudices, and your established ways of achieving self-expression, self-satisfaction, and self-defense. After all, these are the only means you had up to now. Imperfect and un-

satisfactory as they may be, they seem less uncertain and indefinite than any new efforts at self-renewal. Therefore, your nature will tend to hold on to her old ways.

3 Thus, you need not fear your natural reluctance to work toward a truer self-fulfillment through a more realistic self-management. This reluctance is nature's hesitation to expose herself to new experiences which may bring failure, guilt-feelings, and anxiety. Your present ways of responding to life's daily events and situations, have deep roots within your mind and nervous system. Your habits of mind and body are a development that grew through the years. From your first conscious moment, you began life's incessant effort to fulfill the needs and wants of your personal nature. The original simplicity of these needs and wants has long since grown into a complex system of self-expression, self-satisfaction, and self-defense.

4 In proportion as you permit your unreasonable feelings and emotions to dominate your thinking and determine your decisions, you are preventing yourself from any further growth in mind and spirit. You are dooming yourself to live by the feelings and emotions of the past. In a real sense, you are living in

a rut, and are forced to limit your thinking and self-management to the small circle of your self-doubts, insecurity, and anxiety. To live this way, is to live as a child. You will always depend on others to think and decide for you in any matter beyond your habitual, daily experience.

5   With knowledge, time, and patient practice, you can change any rut into a groove. A rut is not made by design. It just happens through a number of chance circumstances. It leads nowhere in particular, and hinders the progress of anyone who would like to decide his own direction and destination. A groove, on the contrary, is a consciously and deliberately constructed channel, leading toward an intended goal. In so far as you can detach your thinking from unreasoning feelings and unrealistic emotions, you are destroying the rut of blind habit. You transform that rut into a groove when you try to base your reason and self-management on objective reality and truth.

6   True, you will not always be fully sure of the reality, facts, or truth that concern you at the moment. At such times, you can seek advice or make a reasonable judgment, and then proceed to act on your decision. Even if

you are objectively mistaken, neither God nor fair-minded people will think the less of you for it. To err is human. Every man makes mistakes at one time or another.

7   Moreover, there may be times when your feelings or emotions are too strong for your intelligent self-management. This too need not be a cause for shame, humiliation, or self-blame. Some habits are so deeply entrenched in your spontaneous behavior that you can only keep trying in the face of repeated recurrences of these habits. If you are willing to continue your effort, God is willing to stand by and help you make progress. The only true failure, whether culpable or not, is the man who surrenders to self-disgust or discouragement.

8   Your general outlook on life today and your attitude toward many things at this moment, depend on your total life-experience. Much of your present behavior proceeds more from habit than from actual self-possession. For this reason, your good intentions and sincere efforts toward a firmer self-determination, will often be interrupted, or at least swayed, by your unreasoning emotions and unwanted habitual feelings. Once you are firmly convinced of this fact, you will find

it easier to persevere in your noble effort to work at a fuller self-possession and more constant self-management. You will gradually cease expecting quick results or perfect achievement in your effort. You will slowly become less and less susceptible to self-disgust and discouragement.

9 Just as your old habits developed and gathered their present strength over a long period of time, so must you be disposed to give time and repeated practice to the new desired habits. For a while, you may feel as though you are merely pretending. You will feel so sure that the old feelings or attitudes are more truly yours than the new intention and effort. God, however, will be more disposed to see the real "you" in your new effort rather than in your old habits. He will acknowledge and respect the "you" you are trying to be, rather than judge you by the unwanted recurring behavior of the past.

10 Not only must you not expect your new effort to flourish fully and perfectly from the start, but you must also expect the old habits to recur in spite of your good will. Your self-renewal cannot be anything but gradual and slow, because you are constantly bucking the strong tide of established habits. They will

make themselves felt especially when you are tired, or emotionally involved with some person, work, or situation. Though you may still "feel" the old way at such times, try to "think" the new way. Eventually, your "new thinking" will engender "new feelings" in line with your growing "new self." Remember, the work of self-development is the work of a lifetime. Jesus said, ". . . the man who stands firm to the end will be saved." (Matt. 10:22) You may not have much visible success to show at the end of this earthly road; but if you have a continued, reasonable effort to show, you will hear the words: "Well done, good and faithful servant; you have shown you can be faithful in small things. I will trust you with greater; come and join in your master's happiness." (Matt. 25:21)

4

Perspective in Daily Life

¹**M**OST people have a strong desire for self-possession, i.e., they want to be their own master, with the right to assume self-command and the ability to maintain self-control. They resent any invasion to their privacy, i.e., their right to experience their

own feelings, think their own thoughts, and make their own decisions without unwarranted interference. This desire is legitimate and inviolable, unless one unjustly disturbs the rights of others or threatens the common good of his fellow-men.

2 Every truly wise man wants his self-expression, self-satisfaction, and self-defense to be correct, i.e., to be in line with reality and truth. He would be disturbed at the thought that he might be deceiving himself, or was open to the justified reproach of others. For this reason he would rather be right than wrong in his daily efforts at self-fulfillment. Only by being right can he be at peace with himself and others.

3 Just as a good motorist has his car checked at reasonable intervals, so does the wise man check on himself from time to time. He is interested in seeing himself as he really is, because he honestly wants to be true to his human nature and personal dignity. His interest, however, is not morbid. He does not blame himself for unavoidable short-comings or unwanted limitations. Neither does he wish to avoid the genuine responsibilities that prove him master of his own life. He lives within his means, i.e., by making

use of the talents, opportunities, obligations, and supernatural graces at his disposal. He sees his natural limitations as God-given limits to his personal achievement. He knows that to seek his fulfillment beyond those limitations, would be a foolish effort and a useless straining.

4 There are people who actually worry about their true worth and about the quality of their daily performance. Some of them turn their daily life into a nightmare of straining for perfection. Others simply give up in despair of ever meeting the ideals and standards which they imagine God expects of them. Too few strike the happy balance of living peacefully within their personal bounds of good will, limited abilities, and peaceful performance. How does one arrive at such a balance amid the complexities of earthly living?

5 Your first step toward organizing a more acceptable self-structure, must be the development of a realistic perspective. A true perspective is more than mere knowledge of the facts. It is a broad and penetrating view of your personal earthly life. It helps you look on the persons, things, circumstances, and situations involving you today, as part of your

total earthly existence and eternal destination. You will see God as the center of the entire panorama, and yourself as the center of your own place in the scene. You will feel some sense of relationship and involvement between yourself and everyone else.

6 Perspective brings clarity to the mind, depth to the judgment, decision to the will and a satisfying orderliness to one's daily performance. It inspires a healthy respect for one's own human dignity, and inclines him to give due respect to his fellow-man. He can look on his own shortcomings without needless shame or harsh self-defense. He can give of himself without feeling exploited, and consider his own needs without feeling guilty of selfishness. In short, perspective helps one achieve a healthy self-acceptance and inclines him toward a reasonable acceptance of others as they are.

7 As your perspective grows in breadth and depth, you will find yourself acquiring a keener awareness of God's presence in your daily round of occupations. Your religious sense gradually becomes so intertwined with your natural interests and concerns, that nature and grace are seen as two hands of God embracing you and sustaining you. With

perspective your passing earthly activities become steps not only toward your natural self-fulfillment in this life, but also toward your unending, all-satisfying self-fulfillment with God in heaven. You will see your personal life on earth as your share in the evolution of God's original act of creation. Whether your personal gifts and opportunities be great or small in the eyes of worldly men, you will see them as a part of God's over-all plan to draw all things back to Himself in due time.

8 The more your balanced perspective develops, so much the more will you realize why a true self-development is the work of a lifetime. It is not a negative self-dismembering analysis, but a positive self-discovering synthesis. The treasure found in the field of which Jesus spoke, is within you. God speaks to you not only through His supernatural grace, but also through the individual nature which He fashioned into the person you are today. He would have you make an intelligent, reasonable use of the gift that is "you."

9 Through a clearer and fuller perspective, you can gradually broaden your view of earthly life so much, that today's "problems" and "crises" will shrink to their proper pro-

portion in your outlook. You will face them more easily and deal with them more calmly, without undue exaggeration, dangerous minimizing, or rash neglect. Such perspective cannot be constructed overnight, nor in a single day, nor even in a week or a month. It takes time to organize the knowledge, deepen the understanding, apply the principles, and learn to accept your nature's pace and limitations. You will gradually become realistic enough to work daily and hourly against old feelings of impatience for results, fear of failure, and guilt for anything less than a perfect achievement.

5

An Invitation to Self-Realization

JESUS did and said many things in His earthly life which were intended not only for the people whom He met at the time, but also for the countless people yet unborn. He is the Way, the Truth, and the Life. His words are the words of eternal life. Without Him no man can come to His Father in heaven. Nathaniel, one of Christ's Apostles, was very skeptical of Him when he first came to Jesus. He was stunned when Jesus told

him that He had seen him under the fig tree,
since Nathaniel was positive that he had had
perfect privacy. This revelation converted
Nathaniel and made him one of Christ's
followers for life. (John 1:45-49)

2   So too, you are no stranger to Jesus. He is
closer to you than you are to yourself. He
understands you better than you understand
yourself. He sees you in your most intimate
thoughts, desires, hopes, fears, discouragement, and hostility. He paid dearly for your
redemption and thereby proved how much
you mean to Him. Your changing moods,
dispositions, and attitudes do not change His
personal concern for you. In fact, your very
sins cannot turn Him away from you. To your
dying day, He will continue to stand by you
because without Him you cannot attain
eternal life. (John 15:4-6)

3   Jesus Himself said, "Come to Me, all you
who labor and are overburdened, and I will
give you rest." (Matt. 11:28) In His words
and example He speaks to you most intimately
and personally, even though you may feel
that you are quite alone and far from God.
He gave you His Church to guide you toward
His Truth, and His sacraments to strengthen
you against your natural weaknesses. Even

when you are in doubt about your personal worth or worthiness, He has no doubts about you. Your value comes not from yourself alone, nor does it depend simply on what you achieve in your daily life. He did more than make reparation for your sins. Through His sacraments, He raised you to a supernatural level of life. In baptism Jesus gave you the supernatural virtues of faith, hope and charity, which you are to develop throughout your daily life. Do not judge your success or failure by visible results alone. In God's eyes, your daily desires, intentions, efforts and general conduct may be more convincing witnesses of your good will than your visible successes. He will take into full account the natural obstacles and limitations that prevented you from achieving greater external results.

4   When the rich young man asked Jesus what he should do to gain eternal life, Jesus told him to keep the commandments. When the young man asked whether he might do more, Jesus told him how he might rise to a higher level of union with God. The young man was not prepared to pay the price and Jesus did not press him beyond his present good dispositions. (Matt. 19:16-22) Jesus

acts the same way with you. He accepts you as you are at present, and then helps you within the limits of your vision and strength of today. Jesus is far more reasonable with you than you are with yourself. He does not expect you to be today the better person you can be next year. It will take you a year to gain the wisdom, prudence and strength which will be yours a year from now.

5   The first qualification you will need to achieve this spiritual development, is humility. Humility is the virtue which disposes a man to: 1) face reality as it is, 2) change what can be changed, and 3) learn to make the most of what cannot be changed. Without humility you cannot live a realistic life. You will only complain without helping yourself, or rebel without regard for the personal rights and justified feelings of others. You will be acting as a child, in spite of your age and experience.

6   Daily spiritual progress involves mental growth and emotional development, as well as the daily use of the supernatural graces at your disposal. Religious knowledge alone will not always be enough to achieve this progress. Some of the situations arising in your daily life, require a fuller knowledge of human

nature itself. Knowing more about your nature, you will gradually understand God more deeply. You will not expect Him to do for you what He has already enabled you to do for yourself. You will no longer separate nature and grace as though nature were evil in itself, and only grace were good. God speaks through nature as well as through revelation. Though man does not live by bread alone, he still needs bread to help him live.

7 Some people find their religious thinking limited, frustrating, or even disturbing. Their supernatural faith seems most alive when they consider the possibility of their being rejected by God. Their supernatural hope is almost powerless against their natural doubts, fears, or disinclination to religious thinking and moral considerations. Their sense of charity is often crowded out by their daily routine or by their habitual negative attitudes toward themselves, other people or God.

8 Every human being has some measure of this basic human problem. However, some people believe in letting sleeping dogs lie. They go along each day making the same mistakes and repeating the same faults from one end of the year to the other. Though God does not push anyone beyond his endurance,

He does expect you to do what little you can each day toward a fuller self-realization. Though you may never be the kind of person you would like to be, you can certainly come a little closer to your goal with a bit of intelligent planning. Even if there be little or no visible growth through the years, at least you can offer Him a persevering daily effort as a sign of your genuine good will.

9 Busy as your daily routine may be, you can fit your effort into the limited time avaliable to you. You might follow this plan: 1) Read a little, 2) Think a little, 3) Apply it to your daily routine, 4) Resolve a little, 5) Practice a little, and 6) Renew your intention when you fail, and begin again. Never count the failures, but rather, count the renewed efforts. This positive attitude will help you maintain a firm determination to *keep trying* for the rest of your life. If you accomplish no more than to avoid the extremes of 1) discouragement, 2) complacency, or 3) rigid attitudes, your effort will be acknowledged by the Lord. In other words, your effort was the best proof of your sincerity and love of God.

6

An Effort Toward Self-Renewal

1 T HE IDEA of self-renewal affects different people differently. Some feel uncomfortable or disinterested at the thought. Consciously or unconsciously, they fear the disappointment, self-doubt, self-blame or punishment which may result each time they fall back into their old ways. Others feel hopelessly weak against some inordinate need or difficult situation in their life. Some people are afraid that God may judge their relapses with the same misunderstanding, narrowness or disgust that others have shown them in their past experience.

2 On the other hand, a number of people are attracted by the idea of self-renewal. It gives them a fresh hope of gaining an uplifting sense of achievement or a feeling of personal worth. Yet, even some of these well-disposed people may go about their self-renewal with a mistaken attitude, unreasonable expectations, and an unrealistic goal. They may view their shortcomings as a proof of laziness or lack of generosity. They may explicitly or implicitly resolve to achieve a self-renewal far beyond their past performance, without realizing that

some of their shortcomings were due to the
God-given limits of their personal nature.
Consequently, their new effort will bear signs
of rigidity in attitude and performance, or an
intolerance of anything short of perfect
achievement. Though they may deny such
unreasonable thinking and unrealistic striving, their denial will be contradicted by their
daily behavior.

3   Man's greatest obstacle in his desire to
accept Christ's invitation, is not always bad
will. God's message and grace must often
contend with misunderstandings and misinterpretations, arising from the past experience, present self-doubts, or anticipated difficulties of each individual. Different people
may read or hear the same religious message
and receive contrary impressions from it. The
very same word or statement can arouse
fear in some people, hope in others, joy in
others, and a positive revulsion in others.
Though they may all be equally intelligent,
each man receives God's message through
the emotional coloring or distortion of his own
individual disposition. Why God permits anyone to misunderstand Him, He alone can say.
On the other hand, He will not blame any

man for what is beyond his limited human powers and supernatural gifts.

4 Whether you are convinced that you are living each day as best you can, or inclined to self-doubts, or apprehensive of God's disapproval, try to live each day with basic "common sense" and a stubborn determination to place your trust in God's fatherly concern for your well-being. He knows only too well the strength of your established habits. He does not encourage a careless attitude in your efforts toward self-renewal. He asks only that you be as reasonable and fair to yourself as you might be to anyone else in the same situation. True, you will need a great deal of self-understanding before you can improve your objectivity toward yourself. In the meanwhile you must also try to understand God better.

5 In this area of self-renewal, God does not expect a sudden change, but rather a gradual growth through a reasonable daily effort. On some days, all you will see is the good intention you made that morning, with no visible success through the rest of the day. On such days, you must simply believe in your own sincerity, renew your intention, and continue your effort as the occasion arises. Jesus is

willing to wait a lifetime for whatever progress you can achieve, be it ever so little. In spite of your self-doubts, simply express a desire to improve, and then do what you can about it.

6 As you go through all this, the world around you will continue being the same old world. The people with whom you deal will still be the same individuals they were before. Their attitudes and habits will still affect you, to some degree, as they did before. Your new effort will consist mainly in trying to follow Christ's teachings more faithfully, though old habits may continue to influence your present thinking and behavior. You will gradually realize that daily living is often a battle against unreasoning needs, wants, and defenses which are well established in you and in the people around you. With grace and persistent effort, you will eventually look upon the old circumstances with a new spirit. External things will gradually bother you less, not because they have changed, but because you have learned to approach them with less self-doubt and less fear of being yourself within reasonable limits.

7 It will not be easy to accomplish this desired improvement in yourself. On the other hand, it is not so hopeless an effort as you may feel. You have to live through the remainder of your earthly life, whether you like it or not. Why not live each day with an intelligent effort to be your own master, instead of being the victim of your unreasoning feelings, moods, and immature attitudes? At least you will have the satisfaction of knowing that you are still trying.

8 In spite of God's grace and your own good will, old habits will recur many times along the way to self-improvement. And yet, amid your inevitable self-doubts, self-disgust or discouragement, Jesus urges you to keep trying. He will not look at your failures half so much as He will at your determination to keep trying. This is not the effort of a day, or month or year. It is the work of a lifetime. Imperceptibly, old faults will weaken and new virtues will grow stronger. Amid the external sameness of things, you will gradually feel a satisfying new sense of personal achievement, a more spontaneous consideration for the human weaknesses and personal shortcomings of others and a heartfelt gratitude for God's fatherly concern for you personally.

7
Self-Understanding in the Effort

1 IN THEIR effort to live each day in closer union with God, some people achieve no more than a mediocre success. This is not always due to bad will, nor to some sinful attachment to the satisfactions of this life. A number of people are hindered from further progress because they lack self-understanding. Though they are aware of their defects or faults, they fail to grasp what is behind these shortcomings. They simply try to control or eliminate them by sheer will power. To their unwarranted shame, disgust or discouragement, they find themselves still falling into the same mistakes or overcome by the same weaknesses. Eventually, they try to distract themselves from their shortcomings or even to rationalize them, i.e., they seek to justify their faults.

2 Self-understanding is more than a mere knowledge of your shortcomings. It looks into these deficiencies and detects the root-causes of them. By working at the root, you may diminish the defect to a minimum. Thus, an impatient man once realized how often his impatience created friction and hostility with-

in himself and those around him. He spent
some time each day considering why he was
so impatient and intolerant when matters
failed to proceed as he desired or expected.
He gradually realized that he was constantly
afraid that he might be exposed to disappointment in himself or open to criticism from
others. For the first time, he really understood his impatience. "He needed to get matters settled as quickly as possible so as to
relax his fear." He eventually diminished his
impatience through his repeated reflections
on the normal imperfections of human nature
and the impossibility of doing all things perfectly. He gradually became "convinced in
practice," that he must learn to accept some
measure of disappointment and criticism as
"normal".

3 Your present emotional tendencies developed through the needs, fears, and dislikes of early life. They became habits,
whether conscious or unconscious. In varying
degrees they still influence your present feelings, thoughts, preferences, and prejudices.
In your present effort to improve yourself,
you cannot begin as though your past never
existed. You must adopt your new goals with

the realization that old habits will continue to interfere for some time to come.

4   Just as it took time and repeated experiences to develop your old ways of feeling, thinking and behaving, so will it take time and repeated efforts to build up your new habits. Unintended lapses into old defects are normal. In spite of your best intentions and sincerest efforts, you will sometimes be taken by surprise or overcome by weakness. Not every fall is a failure. You cannot offend God without some measure of forethought and malice. If you are mature enough to reflect on these falls, and talk them over with God, you will gain greater wisdom and prudence for future occasions.

5   An intelligent self-understanding is not achieved quickly nor easily. In every man there is a natural reluctance to notice or acknowledge short-comings within himself. Consciously or unconsciously, he is afraid of the shame, embarrassment, or self-blame that may disturb whatever interior peace he enjoys at present. To overcome this natural self-defense against anxiety, one needs some measure of maturity.

6   A mature man can be objective enough to realize that the truth is good for him. He is

willing to learn the facts about himself, and to adjust to these facts in order to attain a more orderly self-possession and a more lasting interior peace. He is not prone to doubt his own sincerity, nor will he accuse himself of bad will simply because of his slow pace or repeated failures. When his defects recur, he can 1) Pause briefly, 2) Arrive at a moral estimate of his guilt or innocence, 3) Express his sorrow or thanks to God, and 4) Learn a lesson against future relapses, 5) Then with a renewed determination, he looks ahead, not backwards.

7 With such a mature attitude, you need never fear becoming morbidly introspective. Only the immature are unable to believe in their own sincerity for fear of self-deception. They live constantly in the shadow of their own insecurity, and are burdened by the anxiety it generates. They avoid self-awareness as much as possible, for fear of questioning their own innocence. Some people live in this uneasy state all through life, without ever really understanding what they feel.

8 Self-understanding will take you a long way toward the peace of mind which every man desires. Only the truth about yourself can relieve you of self-doubts in your daily

life. As you advance in self-understanding, you will find contentment in seeing your innocence, and a sincere gratitude in discovering where you may still improve yourself. You will be in a better position to alleviate the inner irritability or interpersonal frictions arising in your daily life. You will more easily correct any unreasonable self-disgust or blind self-defense, as you move slowly toward an intelligent self-acceptance and a truer self-fulfillment.

9 Finally, self-understanding will help you tolerate others more easily. It does this by showing you where others may be right, mistaken or even unjust in their expectations, demands, accusations, or attitudes toward you. In your self-understanding, you will feel strength and peace where you might have felt self-doubt, confusion, anxiety or hostility. You will be more aware of your good will before God. You will eventually be ready to apologize when wrong, and able to justify yourself, at least interiorly, when right.

PART TWO

Man's Basic Dynamism

DIFFERENT as each individual is from all others, there is in every man the same basic root from which spring all of his personality traits. How each man responds to life's daily situations, depends on the mental, emotional, and spiritual habits he developed in his need to achieve self-fulfillment. He has had to compensate for his inadequacy, counterbalance his insecurity, and calm his anxiety. Though all men have had to face this basic inner situation from the very beginnings of life, no two have achieved their respective solutions with the identical set of habits. The infinite variety of personalities in society results from each man's particular solutions to his inadequacy, insecurity, and anxiety.

8. The Nature of Self-Fulfillment
9. Human Inadequacy
10. Man's Basic Insecurity
11. The Problem of Anxiety
12. Anxiety and Self-Fulfillment
13. Anxiety and Hostility in Daily Life

8

The Nature of Self-Fulfillment

1 ANY STUDY of living things reveals sooner or later that whatever possesses the power to live, strives to achieve life as far as circumstances will permit. Who has not seen a lone flower or solitary weed clinging to life in a meager collection of soil on some city street or in the almost invisible crack in some rock or wall? Furthermore, whatever is alive, be it plant, animal, or human, is constantly bent on expressing and protecting its natural powers to grow and develop. Thus, from the tiniest plant to the most cultured human adult on earth, all living things have the common trait of reaching out for whatever can fulfill the needs and appetites of their nature.

2 This drive to self-fulfillment is the most primary and most basic force within you. It stems from your need for biological harmony in your bodily functions, mental and emotional balance in your sense of well-being, and a satisfactory achievement toward those goals and ideals which will bring you your greatest possible self-realization and enduring happiness. Your drive to self-fulfillment

moves you constantly throughout the day. However, whether it moves you toward realistic goals or away from them, depends on the physical, mental, emotional, and spiritual habits you have developed through past experience. A matter-of-fact consideration of this ever-active, all-embracing drive, will help you toward a deeper self-understanding, a more realistic self-acceptance, and a more balanced self-management in your day-to-day living.

3 In your infancy, as long as you were fed, relieved of your physical discomforts, and given some measure of physical closeness and affection, you enjoyed a sense of well-being and contentment. You felt "satisfied, at ease and at peace." You responded favorably to whatever fostered this sense of well-being, and unfavorably to whatever interfered with it. This sense of well-being was the very core of your fulfillment, and you were quick to register your complaint whenever it was interrupted. The first needs of an infant are usually quite elementary and relatively simple. With advancing age, development, and experience, your needs and wants gradually became more complex, and so did your efforts to maintain or restore your

sense of well-being. In these early efforts for interior harmony and contentment, you were already laying the first foundations for your future pattern of behavior.

4   Through the formative years of your childhood, the adults involved in your up-bringing gave you what love and care they could. As you grew out of the helpless infant stage, they endeavored to prepare you for a healthy and orderly life in society. Under the influence of their own personal experience, emotions, knowledge, ideals and graces, they tried to mold you into the kind of adult they felt you should be. Naturally, this training obliged them to direct, inspire, and curb your spontaneous childhood tendencies and inclinations. Many times during this process your sense of well-being was necessarily disturbed.

5   Sometimes you responded to your elders with a willing obedience, sometimes with uncertainty and timidity, and at other times, with some irritation, annoyance or perhaps even hostility. Whatever your contrary feelings, however, your evident dependence on your elders was usually a strong persuader in favor of compliance. How far and how you complied with others depended on which courses of action might best protect your

sense of well-being. This was true even when you were unable to express, satisfy, or defend your more conscious needs, wants or desires of the moment. Your first and deepest need was always to preserve or achieve what satisfaction and contentment you could in the circumstances of the moment. In other words, in proportion as you were able to maintain or restore your sense of well-being, you felt fulfilled as far as you could or dared be at the time. By the time you could assume responsibility for your own life, you had already developed a pattern of emotional, mental, and external behavior designed to hold, regain or defend your sense of well-being and fulfillment.

6   Much as you might like to believe otherwise, you cannot ignore the fact that in this life, man is both united and divided by his very nature. You need no proof of this when you reflect how often you try to think or behave one way, but feel quite the contrary. At such times you are actually aware of operating on more than one level. Though the ideal might be a happy integration of these conflicting tendencies, you have no reason to be ashamed of this division within yourself. It is natural and normal to man. Your problem is

simply how to achieve enough balance between these two levels of striving, to maintain that sense of well-being and self-fulfillment to which you have a right as a human being and a child of God.

7 Everybody, be he saint or sinner, wants to be "somebody." The question is this: Is the "somebody" you want to be, a real, possible and permissible "somebody," or are you reaching for the unreal, the impossible or the forbidden? A true adult reaches for reality, truth and possibility. To do otherwise would be childish or malicious. When St. Paul wrote to the Corinthians about their sacramental elevation into the "Body of Christ," he told them that they could grow in this divine union, through the virtue of charity. He then points out to them that such a growth requires adult desires, attitudes, and efforts. He put it this way: "When I was a child, I used to talk like a child, and think like a child, and argue like a child, but now I am a man, all childish ways are put behind me." (I. Cor. 12:27-13:11) In other words, your real well-being and true self-fulfillment depends on how realistically and maturely you handle the situations of your adult life.

8 Your acquired undesirable habits were

developed through years of striving for self-fulfillment and self-defense. These habits served a real purpose in your earlier life. Now that you have outgrown the ignorance and helplessness of those years, you need attitudes and behavior suitable to your present age, abilities, and responsibilities. Though you may feel that you have achieved this maturity, it cannot do you any harm to make an occasional check-up on your present internal attitudes and responses to the situations and people involved in your daily life.

9 As the human body is constantly building new cells to replace the old, so too can the human spirit renew itself through new insights, new graces, new desires and new efforts. As natural life is a day to day process, so too is the supernatural life of the spirit. They both need time to adjust to life's ever changing circumstances and to adapt themselves to new situations.

10 Possibly the deepest root of your aversion to such an endeavor, is your lack of an adult attitude toward your natural limitations. God respects both your limitations and your personal pace of progress. Being the Author of your nature and Father of your grace, He accepts as a fact, what you cannot control

and what you cannot correct easily or quickly. Perhaps your greatest proof of sincerity and source of merit before God, will be your own stubborn refusal to let discouragement or disgust block your repeated intention and renewed effort after each new failure. If you die trying, you die winning. Your eternal fulfillment and celestial well-being are assured through the blood of Christ, your Savior.

9

Human Inadequacy

1 ANY intelligent effort toward self-fulfillment must necessarily be based on reality, truth and the particular circumstances which constitute your personal life. To most people this statement will seem "too obvious for a second thought." And yet, it is surprising how many human problems arise each day because this "obvious" principle is repeatedly forgotten, neglected or disregarded. A number of people live their daily lives in disgust, disappointment, anxiety or some phase of hostility. They find it hard to adjust to "life as is," and are disinclined to improve, or feel unable to change the circumstances that disturb their sense of well-being.

2 Life around you goes on with or without you. You will find it more interesting and satisfying in proportion as you feel that you are a contributing partner in it. The first obstacle to man's efforts to make his contribution to the world around him, is a "sense of inadequacy." This sense is a feeling that he "may not measure up to what is expected of him" or that he cannot do things "well enough." This "sense of inadequacy" is sometimes very conscious and very definite, but it is more often a rather vague feeling about oneself in general.

3 Every man has his share of this human problem. It is deeply ingrained in your mind, too close for you to recognize it easily, too powerful for you to neglect it altogether. It has contributed to some of your virtues and to a number of your defects. A prayerful consideration of its nature, will help you defend yourself against its undesirable influence on your thinking, decisions and external behavior. Such a consideration will also help you become more understanding and tolerant of the shortcomings within yourself and others. As you grow in this understanding, your daily efforts to maintain your "sense of well-being" through self-fulfillment, will be

more realistic. Why so? Because you will be more disposed to accept your natural limitations and develop your personal talents, such as they are. You can only profit by whatever good lies within your grasp. Your "sense of inadequacy" may prevent you from doing even that.

4 From his first conscious moment, every man finds himself helpless and limited in many things. His dependence on others is painfully evident to him as he cries for the relief and satisfaction of his most basic needs in infancy and early life. All through childhood and adolescence, every human being is subject to his elders for his physical and emotional well-being. Even his ideas and ideals are formed and influenced by his experience with the grown-ups on whom he depends in one way or another. These early-life experiences are further complicated by his associations with other children. As a result, his childhood needs and wants are constantly curbed and frustrated, not only by the expectations of his elders, but also by the needs, wants and demands of his equals. In sheer self-defense, the growing human being forms within himself an idealized image of what he "must" or "should" be, in order

to live in harmony with others, and at the same time feel some measure of peace within himself. Unfortunately, the demands of this idealized self-image can sometimes be more tyrannical and unreasonable than the demands and expectations of others.

5   Thus, by the time the human individual is accepted by society as a responsible adult, he has had a long, convincing experience of his limitations in many things. Though he is now able to "reason" about his "natural limits" and "normal dependence" on others for a number of his daily needs, he cannot quite "feel at ease" about these facts. He cannot eliminate all discomfort over his actual exposure to a possible disturbance or frustration of his sense of well-being. He experiences inner peace only in so far as his sense of well-being seems secure. Every inclination to self-expression, self-satisfaction and self-defense is motivated by this basic need to maintain his sense of well-being.

6   Many people look upon their past life as "over and done with," something quite unrelated to their present personal life. They are not aware of the continuity in human behavior. They do not realize that their present habits are a development from past

experience, which continues to influence present attitudes, outlook, and external conduct. As scars mark a man for life in spite of continual biological changes, so do your early-life experiences continue to leave their mark on your present behavior. In spite of years of schooling and experience, in spite of your present intellectual convictions, moral ideals and supernatural graces, you will always have some likes and dislikes, some prejudices and preferences whose roots reach down to your earliest years of life.

7   Your sense of inadequacy is one of these roots. In so far as you are able to accept your real limitations without shame or self-blame, your sense of inadequacy is no problem. It becomes a problem only when it induces you to strain for what is beyond your grasp, neglect the useful things which are within your reach, or to face life with undue anxiety or unwarranted hostility. You are an adult mentally and emotionally only in proportion as you are willing and able to face facts, build your life within the necessary circumstances that surround you, respect your sincere judgments, and act on your honest decisions. Your neighbor's behavior toward you or thoughts about you, depend far more on

what is inside him than on what you may think, say or do. Though you strain to please, or struggle to convince others of your good will, your influence on them will always be limited by their own inner needs, wants and desires.

8   Being inadequate is a fact of life. You can help yourself only up to a point. From there on, you will need the help of the butcher, the baker, and many other human beings. Beyond these, you will have to cast your needs and your confidence into the fatherly hands of God. Jesus spoke so clearly of His Father's personal concern for you. (Matt. 6:25-34) If you find it difficult to put your trust in God, do not be alarmed. Your sense of inadequacy can sometimes incline you to fear so much for your well-being, as to arouse feelings of insecurity and doubt toward God Himself. You may feel that perhaps God has some reason to test your virtues beyond your endurance, or to punish you severely for the guilt you feel. Such feelings are not necessarily culpable acts of distrust in God. In fact, they are sometimes more forceful, impressive, and convincing than your best objective thinking.

9   At such times all you can do is to profess

confidence in God's divine understanding and hope in His fatherly concern. You may find it hard to make such a profession, because even as you try to express it, you may feel doubtful of your own sincerity or purity of intention. You may feel that you are too concerned with your own well-being, and not enough with God's rights over you. As a result of such self-doubts, you may feel that God won't be "deceived" nor "satisfied" with your profession of confidence. And yet, at that very moment, God will be waiting for you to rise above your doubts and fears by recalling what He Himself revealed through His Prophets, His divine Son, and His Church. God will ask you to accept the fact that His redeeming Son far overpaid the debt of your sins, and outweighed the burden of your guilt. All that remains is, that you declare your faith in Christ's personal merits, your trust in His redeeming grace, and your desire to go on trying, day after day, to follow His words and example within the limits of your human nature and His divine grace.

10   Try to look on your present emotions as a development from past experience. Without being morbid, disgusted, or discouraged, strive to see how your spontaneous feelings

and inclinations tend to influence your clear thinking and wise decisions. Reflect how such behavior is normal to childhood, but not to later life. Gradually, you will grow in mind and spirit. You will slowly achieve something truly wonderful: You will be able to think straight even while your feelings and emotions refuse to face reality, admit truth, or follow facts. Your sense of well-being will be more steady as you develop a larger perspective, that measures things by eternity as well as time. Since it took many repeated experiences through many years for you to develop the undesirable habits that now influence your thinking, do not expect to change such habits overnight. What took years to develop, will require time to change, even with the help of God's ordinary grace.

11   Jesus will not measure your achievement by external results alone. He will have His eye on 1) your intention to try, 2) your determination to keep trying in spite of repeated failures, 3) the effort itself, and 4) the obstacles you meet both within yourself and outside yourself. He simply asks you to "declare your desire," believe in your own sincerity, and then make your effort without undue strain or anxiety. Keep trying, regard-

less of the limited visible results. Do not be impatient with your slow progress, and beware of expecting more than you can achieve this day. As He showed so often in His earthly life, Jesus considers each man's capacity and respects each one's limitations. He walks with him who cannot run, and crawls with him who is unable to walk. Eventually you will find your own proper pace, and you will learn to respect it. Rest assured that Jesus will go along with you, even if you can do no better than take one halting step each day. Even if you fall before that step is completed, Jesus will stand by you and wait understandingly for you to rise again for another try.

10

Man's Basic Insecurity

IN ACCORDANCE with God's divine plan, every man on earth is constantly restricted, in one way or another, by his natural limitations. No man is adequate to solve all the problems, difficulties, or unpleasant situations arising in his daily life. Even if you lived in the best of circumstances, you would still have to tolerate some frustrations, disappointments, failures, and sorrow. In spite of your deepest sincerity and best efforts, you cannot avoid all human errors, misunderstandings, doubts, anxieties, and hostilities.

2   There will always be enough unpredictable factors in your daily life to make you unsure of yourself in many things. Your habitual awareness of this fact, be it ever so vague, implicit, or indirect, generates within you an abiding sense of "basic insecurity." We call it "basic" because it is centered around no particular situation, but around your personal inability to be self-sufficient in all things. Your self-fulfillment cannot always be achieved, and your sense of well-being must necessarily be disturbed from time to time. As a result, with or without your awareness, you will have some measure of uneasiness and tension in a number of your daily activities.

3   Just as your daily behavior is intimately connected with your drive to self-fulfillment, so too is your neighbor's behavior centered around his own similar drive. As your emotions, attitudes, and moods can color or distort your image of others, so too can their mental or emotional operations affect their

image of you. Therefore, in your daily interpersonal relations, do not be surprised if
your good will and sincere efforts are not
always understood, appreciated, or accepted
by those with whom you deal. How well you
tolerate or deal with this interpersonal situation, depends partly on how well you understand and manage your own basic insecurity.
The less sure you are of yourself, the more
will you feel ill at ease or hostile in dealing
with others.

4 Besides your general unsureness of self
and your varying insecurity with other people,
you may also experience, at one time or
another, some insecurity with God. In spite
of His efforts to convince you of His personal
love, understanding, acceptance, and forgiveness, you may occasionally be disturbed
by self-doubts or by a fear of God's rejection.
If these feelings proceed from definite faults
or sins, you can take advantage of various
remedies to restore your sense of well-being.
On the other hand, some of your uneasiness
with God may stem from your basic insecurity. Under the influence of purely subjective
attitudes, you may consider yourself unde-
serving of God's attention, help or pardon.
You may be so doubtful of your own sincerity

or your ability to keep your good resolutions, as to surrender to sheer hopelessness.

5 Normal as some feelings of insecurity may be, you need to guard yourself against their unwarranted negative effect on you. Through prayer and reflection, try to get a fuller understanding of the real harm done to you by uncontrolled feelings of insecurity. The insecure man finds it hard to relax physically and mentally. His doubts and fears interfere with his ability to think clearly and to make an intelligent decision in many things. Even his religious efforts are marked by rigidity, perfectionism, or a tendency to curtail or omit his religious activities as quickly as possible. His mind is more easily distracted from religious occupations than from all other concerns.

6 Insecurity tires the mind with conflicting thoughts, and weakens the judgment with contrary emotions. The victims of insecurity tend to feel like slaves of obligation and duty, rather than like free men and friends of God. They live mostly in anxiety and fear, often in irritability and hostility, and rarely in contentment and love. Their self-fulfillment is unsatisfactory to them, and their sense of well-being is frustrated. The insecure man

presents to the world about him a distorted image of virtue, of religion, and of God.

7 It is important that you understand how deeply insecurity lies within the mind of man. It is not enough that you be impressed by its extreme manifestations. Insecurity operates on many levels of the human mind, in many areas of daily human concern, and in many degrees of human involvement. It can arouse your emotions, formulate your judgments, and inspire your decisions in many things. Much, if not most, of this activity can occur within you long before you become aware that part of you is in disagreement with the principles and ideals you consciously profess.

8 Your way to peace lies along your daily walk of life. Your self-fulfillment must be achieved, not in wishing, but in living each day as it comes. Only in reality can you find your true well-being. As you rise each morning, see your daily routine (and any improvements you can make on it) as your path to eternal glory. Strive to recognize the true values within your grasp, adjust your attitudes to the objective facts of your personal life, and make use of your limited powers within the boundaries of your daily concerns.

If you proceed in this manner from day to day, a year from now you will show forth more wisdom, more contentment, and more godliness within yourself and in your involvements with others. If you simply drift along in insecurity, discontent, and hostility, you will become ever more fixed in the habits which now interfere with your peace of mind.

9 Though you cannot undo all the ill effects of your past experience, you can achieve a considerable self-renewal, with the help of God's grace and your own daily efforts. Your undesirable habits developed through years of repeated misdirected (even if blameless) self-expression, self-satisfaction and self-defense. So too, any attempt at self-renewal will have to follow the same procedure, i.e., repeated daily efforts toward building more wholesome habits, i.e., habits based on objective reality. Observe how your old habits do not tire of repeating themselves over and over again. Then resolve to be just as stubborn, just as determined and just as persistent in building up new attitudes and a new outlook within a new perspective.

10 A wise self-fulfillment respects the unwanted, but inevitable limitations existing within you and within the situations you meet

each day. Reflect often on the facts which must be accepted as a necessary part of your daily life. Familiarity with these facts will help you develop a healthy disregard of them where possible, and an intelligent self-adjustment to them when necessary. Your insight and understanding, assisted by God's grace, will spur you on toward replacing undesirable old habits by developing desirable new ones. Human growth is a life-process, and life is a persistent repetition of nature's constant drive toward self-fulfillment and self-defense. You can play an active part by directing this drive into healthy channels.

11   Christ's teachings are a lamp to your faltering steps. His truth will shine through the darkness of your ignorance and misunderstandings. The example of His earthly life will teach you when mere words fail. His Church will assure you in your self-doubts. His sacraments will give you the light to believe, the determination to keep trying, and the love to prefer eternal fulfillment to any conflicting fulfillment which must one day wane and pass away.

12   Though your past religious performance may have been quite contrary to the preceding description, do not make the mistake of

judging the future by your past experience
alone. God will not expect any sudden,
miraculous transformation in you, unless He
chooses to achieve this by His divine power.
He knows what is in each individual human
soul. He asks only that you seek your fulfillment wisely, with whatever legitimate means
you have at your disposal. Do not let your
image of God be based on previous sad experiences, nor on present misunderstandings
in you and in those around you, nor on your
doubts or anxieties about future commitments.

13 The man who allows his insecurity feelings to distort his thinking and misdirect his
judgments, becomes his own greatest obstacle
to God's grace. In your sincere desire to live
a truthful life, give some thought each day
to the words and example of Jesus. His
example will prevent you from misunderstanding His words. Like so many people who
came face to face with Him, you will gradually find in Him the understanding, acceptance, reassurance and support which will
bring you the sense of security, good-will and
peace for which every man yearns.

II

The Problem of Anxiety

1 AS LONG as you bear the burden of your human inadequacy and insecurity, you will be subject to some measure of anxiety. The supernatural peace which Christ promised to His followers is not intended to eliminate all natural anxiety in your life. Rather, it is a grace that will help you cope, in varying degrees, with the confusion and indecision aroused in you by the conflicting anxieties of daily human living. Man's life on earth is a burden, a warfare, and a glorious challenge. It is a burden because of your inborn drives, basic needs, and acquired wants. It is a warfare because you must daily contend with spontaneous natural appetites and unreasoning emotional tendencies. It is a glorious challenge because you must endeavor to govern and guide your bodily needs, emotional urges, and spiritual leanings with the light of your native intelligence and the power of God's supernatural graces.

2 Your daily life is your path to eternal glory. You have your personal qualities, circumstances, and opportunities. You also have your limitations, both within yourself and in

the situations and people involved in your daily routine. You can refuse to face these facts, by straining beyond your limits, or by surrendering to self-pity, self-excuse, self-blame or unreasoning hostility against others. On the other hand, you can learn to live within your limits and make the most of your talents and opportunities. Which of these courses you choose, depends in good part on your ability to handle the average, natural anxiety of everyday living.

3 Anxiety is nature's immediate response to insecurity. Every living creature has a relentless drive to self-fulfillment. Man is no exception to this first law of nature. He strives in numberless ways, to maintain a sense of well-being through self-care, self-expression, and self-defense. Whatever threatens or hinders this primary drive, immediately arouses insecurity and fear in you.

4 Anxiety is an expression of fear. However, it is not always recognized as fear. It is often felt as a vague, indefinite uneasiness, which you cannot always explain or even understand. It is not a fear of this specific object or that particular person, even though it may seem to be so at the moment. Anxiety is usually centered around one's own sense of

personal inadequacy and insecurity, rather than around any explicit threat or danger. Some measure of anxiety is inevitable in this earthly life. And yet, you are not completely helpless against it. As you understand it more fully, you will find yourself better able to cope with it.

5 Man has known anxiety all his life. In his early years, he was very much aware of his inadequacy and his dependence on others for his well-being. He was not always sure of the approval, acceptance, and assistance on which his sense of well-being depended. Through the years, you have forgotten most of the specific situations that aroused your childhood fears, but each situation has left its impression on your mind and nervous system. By now, you are so accustomed to your personal anxiety that it often influences you without your slightest awareness of it. You may simply feel some measure of bodily tension, nervousness, mental uneasiness, or an unaccountable reluctance to face some situation or person. You may even feel like "striking out" at others in thought, word, or deed. It may not occur to you that your mind and body are being disturbed by a long-standing habit of anxiety. Your un-

awareness leaves you almost defenseless against this enemy of your interior peace.

6　Anxiety is not only a hindrance to your natural well-being, but it is also an obstacle to the ordinary effectiveness of God's grace in you. It really interferes with your religious thinking and your personal efforts to achieve a greater degree of self-possession. Since anxiety often remains hidden from your awareness, you must learn to recognize its symptoms. When you cannot give any intelligible reason for being tired, depressed, tense, restless, bored, irritable or the like, you could be feeling the effects of unconscious anxiety within you.

7　Every man has to face some situation or other that may be somewhat new or unfamiliar to him. If he is realistic, he will do what he can about it and respect himself for his effort. He will scorn his childish fear of imperfect results, or the possible rash judgments of others about his effort. The wise man accepts his natural inadequacy, even though he does not like it. He lives within his limitations, and makes the most of his talents and graces, though he might wish to do better or to achieve more. Being realistic about his capacities, he tries to tolerate the unreasoning insecurity he feels in his effort. He is neither too proud to ask for help, when necessary, nor is he unduly ashamed to admit his limitations, when such is the case. He sees the unfavorable attitudes and opinions of others as legitimate expressions of their personal viewpoint or as consequences of their own personal problems. This realistic and wholesome outlook on life can help you eliminate some of your natural anxiety, diminish some of it, and tolerate the inevitable minimum that lies deeply rooted within every human being.

8   Your effort to reduce your natural anxiety, will be a slow process at first. This habit of fear will be more stubborn in its recurrence than your efforts to overcome it. Simply expect this to be the case, and you will not easily be swayed by the immature urge to demand more of yourself than you can achieve for the present. Refuse to give up your effort because of discouragement or disgust. The change will begin with an effort to "think with the facts." You will fail many times. This is to be expected, since nature tends to follow her basic drives and acquired habits, rather than your intellectual insights and moral good intentions. Slowly your realis-

tic convictions will become stronger against
the emotional thinking that dominated your
life in the past.

9 Keep your eyes on your efforts, and leave
the "failures" in Jesus' hands. Remember, in
His own mysterious way, He too bore the
burden of anxiety on earth, e.g., during His
agonizing prayer in the Garden of Olives.
Stubbornly continue your effort to achieve an
intelligent, supernatural self-possession. Jesus
will gradually show you how His divine peace
can be enjoyed even while your natural
anxiety continues to make its presence felt.
You will eventually see how you can "feel
afraid," without "thinking fear" or acting
upon its childish impulses. You will gradually
enjoy more of the freedom of the sons of God.

12
Anxiety and Self-Fulfillment

1 AS YOU study God's ways in your human
nature, you will perceive ever more
clearly that anxiety plays a central role in
your everyday life. With or without your
awareness, anxiety influences your feelings,
thinking, preferences, prejudices, attitudes,
and outlook in numberless situations. It does

the same to the people involved in your daily life. Thus, people often sense some uneasiness or tension within themselves or others, without quite appreciating the meaning of these stresses. As a result, they sometimes find themselves unfavorably disposed toward themselves or others for no apparent good reason, or for reasons that are either totally or partially misunderstood, misplaced or misdirected.

2 It would help you immensely toward a greater internal peace of mind and external harmony with others, to reflect often on the basic human problem: It is normal for man to experience some measure of emotional stress, not only in his dealings with others, but also in his self-directed concerns and expectations. Why is this so? Every man has his share of inadequacy feelings. Be they ever so vague or indirect, these feelings of inadequacy arouse some sense of insecurity. From this sense of insecurity, proceeds some degree of anxiety. He who would live at peace with himself, God, and his fellow man, must learn to tolerate the inevitable anxieties of this earthly life.

3 Anxiety is at the root of many a human problem. This is so because anxiety is intimately related to man's most basic drive, i.e.,

self-fulfillment. This is nature's first and
most all-embracing drive. From it stem all of
nature's inclinations to satisfy its inborn
needs and acquired wants. Self-fulfillment
brings man a sense of well-being. Only with
this sense does one feel reasonably satisfied
with himself and tolerably content with life.
No matter what your conscious motives or
deliberate intentions may be, your nature
will tolerate no frustration, threats, or inter-
ruptions in this all-important sense of well-
being. Nature's immediate response to any
such interference, is anxiety. When anxiety
is aroused, it musters nature's energies of
mind and body to defend or restore her sense
of well-being. The more acute the anxiety,
so much the more does the situation become
a matter of survival. Nature is inclined to
avoid the danger, if possible, or fight the
threat if necessary. However, whether by
flight or fight, some solution must be applied.

4   The particular means by which one
achieves, maintains, defends or regains his
sense of well-being, will vary with each
individual. Since each man's life history is a
personal experience, the needs and wants
he must satisfy, and the manner, degree and
complexity with which he tends to satisfy

them will have its own personal character. No two persons have quite the same constellation of preferences, prejudices, fears, or hates. Though all men have the common trait of seeking to fulfill, defend or restore their sense of well-being, each individual does so through habits he has developed in his own past experience.

5 Thus, each day you face life with your particular personality traits. These traits are for the most part, the habits you developed through the years, to achieve your self-fulfillment, and to allay those stresses of anxiety which disturbed your sense of well-being. These habits are no longer the simple self-expressions or evident defense mechanisms of childhood, but intricate refinements of your successful solutions against whatever aroused your anxiety through the passing years.

6 These habits help you only in so far as they are in accord with external reality, intelligent thinking, and God's revealed truth. In so far as they misrepresent or disregard the objective facts, your habits of self-satisfaction, self-expression, or self-defense can hurt you and people involved in your everyday life. Though you cannot achieve a complete reno-

vation of your personality habits, you can improve your self-fulfillment and sense of well-being through an enlightened good will and the help of God's grace.

7 The supernatural gifts which God bestows on you, do not destroy your individual nature. Rather, they raise your nature to a higher level of thinking, yearning, and endeavor. Even on this higher level, however, each person is still seeking the fulfillment and preservation of his sense of well-being. God's gift of faith extends man's outlook beyond the limits of this earthly existence. The divine gift of hope urges man to reach out for an undying self-fulfillment in spite of his disturbing human limitations and personal shortcomings. The supernatural gift of charity enables man to perceive his greater well-being where bodily eyes cannot see and natural reason cannot penetrate.

8 On the other hand, God's grace does not usually perform miracles. It fosters your supernatural life within the limited framework of your personal nature, and operates within the narrow channels of your personal habits of body, mind, and spirit. In its own mysterious way, God's grace influences your emotional formation, intellectual growth,

physical energies and moral development. At the same time, these same elements of your personal nature, have their own limiting effect upon the graces you receive from God. Consequently, the infused virtues flowing from God's grace in you, are helped or hindered by the natural habits you have developed through the years.

9 The person you are today, took years to develop into the personality you possess at present. There is much that you know about yourself, and much that you know only partially or not at all. What inclines you to behave as you do is your particular way of achieving self-fulfillment and self-preservation. If you let your feelings and emotions alone guide your thinking and behavior, you will remain a child, or worse, all your life. If, on the other hand, you try to base your thinking and self-management on reality, truth and God's grace you will be a true adult, whatever your natural limitations or defects may be.

10 God does not expect you to neglect your legitimate needs and wants. He does not ask that you live only for the life to come. The nature He created in you would rebel at such a thought. God wants you to strive for

your earthly well-being as best you can with whatever legitimate means you have at your disposal. On the other hand, He does expect you to strive for your earthly well-being with intelligence, reasonableness, and a realistic acceptance of the natural and supernatural limits that mark your personal boundaries. God's creation is much too complex for you to understand its intricate operation. Much that you may be inclined to question now, will be made clear to you in God's own good time. In the meanwhile you have a choice of "kicking against the goad" like Saul of Tarsus, later known as St. Paul, (Acts 26:14); or you may endeavor to make the most of life as it comes to you today.

11　　No matter what extremes your anxiety may suggest to you, your true well-being can only be achieved in reality as it is at the moment. Much as you may strive for the fulfillment of your needs and the satisfaction of your wants, you will achieve only a limited success in your motives and goals. It will help you keep your natural anxiety in control, if you can see your limited achievements as your personal contribution to God's work on earth. As each member of a team contributes to the ultimate success of the whole team, so will your limited personal fulfillment help the community of which you are a part. Whatever your present dissatisfaction or disappointment in yourself or your life thus far, it will be alleviated in proportion as you appreciate the total picture of your personal life. Your present life is a significant part of your eternal life, just as each hour on earth is part of your entire existence both here and hereafter.

12 No matter how satisfying or difficult your earthly life is, you have God's own word that the best is yet to be. Reflect often on the vision which God granted to St. John the Evangelist: "Then I saw a new heaven and a new earth; the first heaven and the first earth had disappeared now, and there was no longer any sea. I saw the holy city, and the new Jerusalem, coming down from God out of heaven, as beautiful as a bride all dressed for her husband. Then I heard a loud voice call from the throne, 'You see this city? Here God lives among men. He will make his home among them; they shall be his people, and he will be their God; his name is God-with-them. He will wipe away all tears from their eyes; there will be no more death, and no more mourning or sad-

ness. The world of the past is gone.' Then the One sitting on the throne spoke: 'Now I am making the whole of creation new,' he said. 'Write this: that what I am saying is sure and will come true.' And then he said, 'It is already done. I am the Alpha and the Omega, the Beginning and the End. I will give water from the well of life free to anybody who is thirsty; it is the original inheritance of the one who is victorious; and I will be his God and he a son to me.' " (Revelation 21:1-7)

13 Though God Himself inspired St. John to put this vision into words, your natural sense of inadequacy, insecurity, and anxiety can make you deaf to his words and blind to his vision. Nature is usually felt more strongly than the gifts of grace, but grace speaks the more lasting and more reliable facts. Your daily conflict is often a battle between how you feel about life and how God would help you think about it. Pray and labor to build up so strong a faith and trust in God that you would rather deny your own emotional ideas than God's message of Divine Love. He loves you not because of the smallness you see in yourself, but because of the supernatural greatness bestowed on you through the labors and merits of His divine Son.

14   This vision of the Evangelist was not intended to minimize your earthly life. On the contrary it emphasizes the true greatness and ultimate of glory of your present daily commitments. Created by God, you must one day return to Him. During the interval between your entrance into this world and your departure from it, God offers you a glorious opportunity to improve His work of creation. You do this by your intelligent, reasonable and grace-inspired handling of the persons, things, and circumstances involved in your personal life. For better or worse you will leave your mark upon the world. Your true self-fulfillment will be achieved in proportion as you try to live this life with the attitudes, outlook and self-management of an adult, i.e., a person who tries to help himself with the help of God.

13

Anger and Hostility in Daily Life

¹FROM your first waking moment to your last conscious thought of the day, your drive to self-fulfillment moves you from one concern or interest to another. This drive inclines or spurs you toward the satisfaction of

each succeeding need or want. With each fulfillment you enjoy some sense of well-being. In proportion as fulfillment is blocked or interrupted, you experience some measure of emotional turmoil, bodily tension, and mental frustration. The more intense your need or want, and the more acute your tension and frustration, so much the more easily or totally does your nature respond with anger at the situation.

2 Anger can sometimes be a helpful and desirable emotion. On occasion, it may even be necessary, to help you achieve your legitimate self-fulfillment in difficult circumstances. When properly balanced by a personal sense of justice, your anger disposes you to fight for truth and right order, even in the face of frightening opposition. In such instances, your righteous anger can make the difference between the hero and the coward in you.

3 On the other hand, anger can also be harmful and undesirable at times. Though it always arises as an expression of legitimate self-defense, it can sometimes be blindly unreasonable and utterly unjust in its effort to remove pressing needs or fulfill mounting desires. Whether it comes as a mild annoy-

ance or as an open hostility, anger can create more disorder and misery than the situation warrants. This is understandable when you consider that nature's first instinct is, to withdraw in fear when faced with a threat to her well-being. Only when flight is impossible and the mounting anxiety, tension and frustration become intolerable, does nature respond with anger. With fear and anxiety oppressing the mind, chemical changes occur within the body, and nature's sense of well-being is shattered. In this state of urgency, nature confronts the threat with hostility. She may direct her hostility inwardly against herself or outwardly against others, depending on what appears as the quickest, easiest or most acceptable solution to the situation.

4 Unfortunately, a person in the state of anger is usually more concerned with restoring his sense of well-being than with the means or manner of achieving this restoration. In other words, he is more disposed to act first and think about it later, rather than pause in the heat of anger and consider what would be his wisest course of action. Only the self-possessed man is able to think realistically under the inner pressure of his

emotions. He is not necessarily less angry
than others, but he is more in command of
his intelligence and good will, in spite of his
emotional involvement. In proportion as he
is able to see the situation in the light of
reason and right order, he is disposed to
guide his judgment and direct his feelings by
the objective facts, circumstances and principles of the case.

5 For all your good will, you will always
have some limitations and defects. No matter
how much you may desire and try to accept
life as it comes, there will always be somebody or something that can annoy you to
some degree. This does not mean that you
cannot grow in self-possession, exercise a
fuller self-management, and achieve a richer
self-fulfillment when your emotions threaten
to overpower your mind. It simply means
that there is an area of your nature that
remains unimpressed by your good intentions
and sincere efforts. In other words, you cannot always determine or command what you
shall think, imagine, or feel about things.
Often enough you will have to fight against
unwanted thoughts, fantasies and feelings.
You can, however, develop a firmer faith in
your own good will, when your spontaneous

behavior does not concur with your chosen principles and ideals. The self-possessed man can do this without becoming a defeatist. He insists on believing that "what he is trying to be or do" is more to his credit than "what he has failed to achieve." He also insists on believing that God is at least as big and understanding as that. This act of faith in your own good will and God's fatherly understanding, will not come easily at first. You will have to contend for some time with the usual obstacles to your healthy growth toward a broader self-possession.

6 The first of these obstacles is your natural sense of inadequacy. You may feel that you are attempting a rather hopeless task. Your judgment may be based on past failures in your efforts to "change" or "improve." The very thought of trying again, may draw little response from you. You may feel reluctant to face more straining efforts, poor results, disgust, discouragement, and guilt-feelings. This prospect would surely incline you to forget the idea of self-possession, and just go on living from day to day, hoping for the best. On the other hand, if you can believe that "trying and failing" is better than "not trying at all," you may yet undertake a new effort.

In fact, you may, with God's help, learn to be grateful for whatever little visible success you can achieve.

7   The second obstacle to your daily growth in self-possession, is your habitual sense of insecurity. You may feel unsure as to how much of your limited achievement "might have been better," if only you had "tried a little harder." Then again, you may feel annoying doubts about God's view of your imperfect performance. "Maybe He sees you as guilty, rather than just plain limited. If so, you are a hopeless mess and a lost cause." So speaks the rigid insecurity of some people. They eventually doubt the good will by which they sincerely desire to live. Their insecurity even affects their relations with other people. They may feel inclined to escape the discomfort, tension or frustration of self-doubts, or avoid their painful sensitivity to the questionable attitudes, judgments, and external behavior of others. Under the above pressures, nature is too preoccupied with self-defense to direct any energy toward a positive self-possession and intelligent self-management.

8   Another obstacle to a realistic self-possession, is anxiety. Some people are so afraid of losing control of their thoughts, fantasies,

feelings, desires, or external behavior, that they maintain a rigid alertness of mind, and caution in what they read, see, think, say or do. Their attitudes and outlook are fixed in a narrow frame of reference and a rigid pattern of behavior. Their frame of reference is one of fear, e.g., fear of falling short of their ideal; fear of deserving criticism, rejection, disapproval or punishment. Their actual self-possession is far from realistic. It is controlled by vague fears, physical tensions, and mental frustrations, rather than by objective reality. Their self-possession is a pattern of self-defense, rather than a satisfying expression of their positive spontaneous drives, expansive emotional fulfillment, and uplifting spiritual aspiration.

9   Is it any wonder that the last inner obstacle to self-possession is anger and hostility? Nature can take the pressures of inadequacy, insecurity, and anxiety only for a limited time. When her endurance has diminished below a certain level, nature lashes out in anger and hostility. True, the endurance of each individual varies from that of everyone else. Moreover, one can improve his endurance of hardship, pain, and privation through self-discipline. And lastly, each man's super-

natural gifts of grace may extend his endurance beyond their natural limits. But sooner or later, each one reaches the end of his endurance. When this occurs, nature's usual tendency is to rally to the defense of her sense of well-being. Whether in a panic of fear or a rebellion of anger and hostility, the preponderant concern of human nature is self-defense. At this point, one must fight against a complete take-over of his irrational emotions.

10   Thus, life seems to be a constant competition between one's unthinking drives, urges and emotions on one side and a reasonable self-management on the other side. Self-possession can make the difference between governing oneself with due regard for facts, and surrendering blindly to unwise needs, wants, fantasies and feelings. Self-possession is another name for "keeping in touch with life's essential realities, truths and principles." One who lives with this broad perspective, is like a true seaman, who steers his craft by the stars and manages it deftly against contrary winds and waves. Such a person is more inclined toward a wise use of his natural gifts and a humble acceptance of divine guidance, rather than follow the un-

realistic whims of chance, guess-work and wishful thinking.

11   Pray daily as though your future were entirely dependent on God; and then proceed to work for your reasonable needs and intelligent desires as though their fulfillment depended entirely on you. In proportion as you see your daily life as a partnership with God, you will find life's inadequacies, insecurities, and anxieties less confusing to the mind, less oppressive to the body and less frustrating to the spirit. Your inadequacies will be counterbalanced by your supernatural faith in God's divine plan for you. (Matt. 25:14-23) Your natural sense of insecurity will find strength in Christ's sermon on His Father's divine providence for His children (Matt. 6:25-34). Finally, your spontaneous anxieties will find solace and peace in the good news of your Redemption. (John I:1-14) This large perspective will make anger and hostility less necessary to you, since your fulfillment will no longer be restricted to the narrow fulfillment of an hour, day or year. Rather, it will be viewed as a noble effort of your grace-dignified human nature, for a reasonable fulfillment on earth and a glorious fulfillment with God in eternity.

PART THREE

The Conflicts of Earthly Life

TRY as he may, no man can avoid all conflicts in this life. Conflicts are a normal part of his daily human efforts to achieve a satisfactory self-possession, self-management, and fulfillment. We see this most clearly when we consider the four basic conflicts of everyday living. Every man experiences some measure of these conflicts in a thousand ways as he goes along his earthly path to his eternal fulfillment. He may not always be aware of these conflicts, nor always understand them when they occur within him, but they are there. Facing them is the first step to solving some and alleviating others.

14
Daily Human Conflicts

¹AS YOUR understanding of human nature broadens and deepens, you will marvel at the constant interplay of simplicity and complexity in your daily efforts toward self-fulfillment. In every tendency, thought, word or action, your nature's primary goal is the achievement of the fullest possible sense of well-being. In contrast to this simplicity of purpose, your nature is also moved by a complexity of needs, wants, feelings, emotions, motives and intentions, which make themselves felt in 1) your body, 2) your imagination and emotions, 3) your rational thinking and moral decisions and 4) your grace-inspired religious endeavors.

2 By your nature, you are inclined to reach out for a sense of well-being and to sustain it as best you can. In other words, you are constantly inclined toward the fulfillment of your wants, your internal peace of mind, and a satisfactory harmony with the people around you. How much and how well you achieve these goals, depends on a number of factors. Some of these factors are entirely within your management; others are only

partially so; and still others are utterly beyond any control of yours. Due to the nature, variety and complexity of your needs and wants, you cannot avoid occasional clashes between them, whether within yourself alone or between yourself and others.

3   This is one of man's greatest problems in this earthly life. Though you have power to think rationally, i.e., to grasp the nature, meaning, and value of things, you also have lesser appetites which are not concerned with greater importance or higher values. Much as you may wish to guide your daily life along the paths of intelligence, reason and divine grace, you will, sooner or later, encounter contrary feelings and wants within yourself. These are just as much a part of you as your higher aspirations and efforts. These lesser wants can sometimes assert themselves so strongly as to be momentarily irresistible. Thus, to a starving man, food is usually his most urgent need. To one who is dying of thirst, water is more precious than gold. In varying degrees, your felt needs and wants make their demands on you, regardless of any contrary desires which you may have at the moment.

4   A conflict arises within a person when his

contrary needs, wants, or desires are somewhat equal in strength. Thus, you may wish
to be helpful to others, but also afraid of some
rejection or failure in your effort. In such
instances, your sense of well-being will be
disturbed in both directions by feelings of
insecurity, anxiety and tension. Your basic
drive to self-defense will urge you to reach
out for whatever solution is more available or
acceptable at the moment. This solution may
be reasonable or not, but it won't usually be
an act of cool, calm decision.

5   God Himself will not find fault with you
when your clarity of mind and calmness of
decision are limited by the tension of need,
the pressure of want, or the inhibitions of
anxiety. He Himself guides your nature by
the laws of self-fulfillment and self-defense.
He knows only too well that you are constantly moved in body, mind and spirit by
your needs, wants, and fears. He also knows
that you can give of yourself only in proportion
as you see value, i.e., some form of fulfillment
or satisfaction, in the giving. The man who
dies for what he loves, does not feel that he
is losing something, but that he is gaining
something in giving his life.

6   Your needs, wants and desires are rooted

in your human nature. They reach for their fulfillment through the habits you developed through the years. They are also influenced toward a truer balance by the light and inspiration of God's supernatural grace. As your needs and wants make themselves felt, they generate your drives, urges and inclinations, which in turn arouse your feelings, emotions and desires. This process is not always simple or clear to you. It is often only partially conscious or totally unconscious. Your spiritual needs and wants are sometimes so interpenetrated with natural feelings and yearnings that you cannot be sure which level of your being is inspiring your motives and intentions. No matter which way you choose or decide at such times, you may still feel some inclination toward the opposite.

7   Though you may try to live with the highest motives and the best of intentions, you will always be subject to some conflicting wants, mixed desires and doubtful intentions. This is the normal state of man on earth. You must be realistic enough to accept this fact. Being human, you have to bear your share of internal and external conflicts in this life. You may sometimes misunderstand yourself in these conflicts. When your spontaneous

feelings are averse to performing some necessary activity or some good deed, it does not necessarily mean that you have bad will. It can mean any number of things. You may be overly tired, preoccupied with some pressing concern, or burdened with some unresolved anxiety. Try to see these situations in their total perspective. This will help you understand the true meaning of your inner conflict.

8   Your daily life is not always a simple matter of "right or wrong," "good or evil." Your nature reaches out spontaneously for fulfillment in her variety and complexity of drives, urges, needs and wants on different levels. Your body wants rest when tired, even though you may want to work on toward a worthy goal. Your feelings will not always agree with your logical thinking, nor will they always submit to your grace-inspired efforts toward a desirable ideal. And yet, though you may know in theory that this is quite natural and normal, you may still be inclined to judge yourself unfairly.

9   In a sense, conflicts are necessary for the balanced development of man in his present state on earth. He is born utterly helpless and dependent. He needs a good deal of instruc-

tion, practice and grace, to manage his own affairs in due time. With God's help you can gradually acquire a fuller self-possession and self-determination, and improve your daily contribution toward the development of the world around you. Human conflicts will sometimes interfere with your efforts. If, however, you concentrate only on your moments of hesitation, temporary helplessness, or imperfect achievement, you may easily underestimate how well you actually did against the obstacles in your way. You may fail to see that you probably achieved as reasonable a solution and as commendable a performance as was possible in the total situation.

10   Though you may agree intellectually that conflicts are quite normal to daily human living, each new conflict will continue to arouse some measure of insecurity and anxiety in you. Even when you are fully aware of your contrary needs, wants and desires, some feelings of discomfort and uneasiness will accompany each conflict until it is resolved. These feelings tend to interfere with your efforts to: 1) think clearly, 2) judge accurately, and 3) make a realistic decision.

11   Even when you have made such a decision, you will sometimes continue to ex-

perience some doubt or fear that you may not have chosen wisely or generously enough. This state of mind is understandable, considering the nature of your inner conflicts. Every conflict presents a choice between two alternatives which are about equally desirable or equally disturbing. In each conflict you experience some degree of tension and some measure of frustration, since the choice of one alternative usually involves the exclusion of the other. In spite of your sincere desire to exercise a more englightened self-management, your nature will reach anxiously for the shortest way out of the conflict. The shortest way often turns out to be the well-trodden path of past habits. In your present efforts for a greater self-possession, you would be wise to reflect more fully on: 1) the sources of human conflicts, and 2) the undesirable solutions which your nature may spontaneously choose in spite of your good will.

12   If you can look on this inner conflict as a "natural and normal" condition of your human nature, you will be less confused, upset, or discouraged when these situations occur. In spite of shortcomings or failures, you will still believe in your good intentions and in the sincerity of your efforts. You will

not hesitate to trust in God's fatherly understanding. You will exercise your supernatural hope by continuing to desire and expect God's acceptance of whatever effort you were able to make. When you find yourself somewhat doubtful about your inner strength of faith or hope, look on this condition as part of your natural self-doubts. Reflect often on St. Paul's inspired message: ". . . We must never let go of the faith we have professed. For it is not as if we had a high priest who was incapable of feeling our weaknesses with us; but we have one who has been tempted in every way that we are, though without sin. Let us be confident, then, in approaching the throne of grace, that we shall have mercy from him and find grace when we are in need of help." (Heb. 4:14-16)

13   Like Paul, you too must become deeply impressed by the fact that Jesus redeemed us by becoming as truly human as we are. Only in this way could He convince us of His "human closeness, sympathy, friendship, and personal concern." He inspired Paul to describe Him in this way: "During his life on earth, he offered up prayer and entreaty, aloud and in silent tears, to the one who had power to save him out of death, and he sub-

mitted so humbly that his prayer was heard. Although he was Son, he learned to obey through suffering; but having been made perfect, he became for all who obey him the source of eternal salvation . . ." (Heb. 5:7-9) As He took our place in His work of redemption, so does the Father see Him in us when we are in need of divine assistance. Whatever your doubts, they are far outweighed by the merits of Christ. Though your daily efforts to live wisely may be ever so imperfect, the merits of Christ will supply what you cannot provide. He asks of you the only thing you can promise, namely to go on trying to live as best you can in spite of your shortcomings and failures. You are to prove your trust in His merits by your refusal to surrender to your doubts or strain beyond your strength.

15
External Sources of Human Conflicts

1 AMID his sufferings, Job exclaimed: "Is not man's life on earth nothing more than pressed service, his time, no better than hired drudgery?" (Job 7:1) To some people this view of earthly life presents a gloomy picture with which they agree. To others, on

the contrary, it presents a challenge which they accept. They are disposed to live each day as it comes. Though they do not expect heaven on earth, neither do they by-pass any reasonable chance to make life a bit more satisfying for themselves and others. They are realistic enough to accept their evident limitations, but they are also disposed to work out their problems—alone if possible, and with help, if necessary.

2 Try as you may, you cannot avoid all conflicts in this earthly life. Between your personal needs, wants and limitations, and those of others, you will have to face some conflicts from time to time. The deeper your understanding of these conflicts, the better your chances of maintaining a broad perspective of the conflict. With a proper perspective, you will achieve a fuller self-possession, a wiser self-management, and a more realistic solution in your conflicts. Knowledge alone cannot achieve this mental, emotional and spiritual growth. Knowledge can be acquired as mere memory, without ever being absorbed into your inner feelings, positive attitudes, sense of values, and healthy involvements. Prayerful reflection will bring you a deeper and richer understanding and apprecia-

tion of what you already know from memory.

3   Children value things in proportion as these things make them "feel" satisfied and content. Mature adults, on the contrary value, things in proportion as these things make a realistic contribution to their true well-being. Your true well-being depends on "how things really are" rather than on "how you feel about them." Though you may dread the extraction of a tooth, you will accept the ordeal, once you realize that further neglect could cause greater harm. So too is it with the unavoidable conflicts of daily life. Everybody dislikes conflicts. When, however, a conflict must be faced, the mature person tries to deal with it realistically, i.e., with due consideration of all the available facts. Though he may experience some insecurity and anxiety, he tries to be as open-minded and fair about the objective situation as he can.

4   The sense of well-being of the brute beast is immersed in his sensible life. The animal lives entirely on its feelings. Even its emotions are different from those of human beings. Unlike the brute beast, man can reflect on his spontaneous emotions. He can evaluate them in so far as they are or are not in accordance with his knowledge, his reason, his

faith, and the objective situation at hand. With proper motivation, man can choose to disregard his unthinking feelings and control the tendencies of his unreasoning emotions. On his spiritual level of life, he can experience emotions which proceed from an intelligent appreciation of truth, goodness, and beauty that far surpass the level of his sense life. He can also make rational judgments of the moral worth of the things he values. Though his sense appetites may clamor for satisfaction without regard for right order, man can perceive his true well-being on a larger scale. With this larger perspective, he can think independently of what he feels, and can choose goals and satisfactions opposed to what he wants on his physical and emotional level of life.

5   The fuller your understanding of human conflicts, so much the broader will your perspective be. The deeper your appreciation of life's true meaning, so much the more balanced will your judgment be in your internal and external conflicts. You will not hesitate to favor yourself when you see yourself in the right. Neither will you be overly reluctant to favor others when you see yourself as mistaken or downright wrong. More-

over, you will be quite aware of the mental
and emotional forces which are prejudicing
you and those at odds with you. Though you
may not know all the answers, you will have
enough appreciation of human nature's internal problems to restrain your spontaneous
inclination to defend yourself at any price.

6   This balanced attitude toward life's daily
conflicts will make you hesitate to pass rash
judgments on those whose vision of life is
restricted by ignorance, emotional doubts,
basic insecurity, and upsetting anxiety. At
the same time, it will make you aware of your
own emotional tendencies to disregard the
truth or to distort it in your own favor. When
self-defense is required, you will perform it
with a desire to help not only yourself, but
also your opponents as far as this is possible.
You will refuse to lose your self-possession by
speaking more emotional than rationally, or
by surrendering blindly to your anger and
resentment. Your balanced view of the situation will incline you to maintain good will
toward your adversaries. It will help you see
these people as victims of their own emotions
rather than as wilfully malicious enemies. In
spite of your own aroused emotions, you will
insist on maintaining possession of your own

clear thinking and deliberate self-management.

7 Is this ideal possible? Can this wonderful self-fulfillment be achieved in this earthly life? After all, you do have your established emotional habits which respond to conflict spontaneously and without sufficient reflection. Natural development alone would not be sufficient for such a marvelous control and management of your natural needs, wants, and emotions. You will need the supernatural strength which God grants to those who have accepted His divine Son as their loving Redeemer and source of supernatural life. The "Good News" of Christ, together with His supernatural gifts of faith, hope, and charity will raise you above the narrow boundaries of natural knowledge, emotional habits, and earth-bound appetites. Only this God-given vision can enlarge your spirit with a strength that surpasses the power of your natural drives, urges, and habits. Endowed with this supernatural inspiration and desire, you will exclaim with Saint Paul: "There is nothing I cannot master with the help of the One who gives me strength." (Phil. 4:13)

8 Inspiring as the above message may be, it is a source of discouragement to some and

of skepticism to others. Some people feel that they have failed God because they have not made "full use" of His supernatural gifts. They think in terms of perfect or quick achievement. To them anything less is somehow displeasing to God. There are others who feel that such a supernatural ideal is impossible to mortal men. They see themselves following their natural needs, wants, and habits with far greater ease and satisfaction than they experience in religious endeavors. It does not occur to these people that they may be misunderstanding the meaning or method of Christ's "Good News." They interpret every natural negative feeling, emotion, inclination, or action as a positive "sin." They see their natural habits in conflict with their supernatural desires or efforts, and interpret these conflicts as proof of bad will. They are mistaken in their understanding and interpretation of these conflicts.

9 Though your re-birth in Christ brings new dimensions to your natural human powers, it does not work as a sudden visible miracle. God respects His natural creation. He does not destroy it by His supernatural gifts. Rather, He elevates it to a higher plane of living. On this level, your natural habits

still make themselves felt. They need to be changed or redirected into healthier channels, with the help of your supernatural gifts.There is a basic law of nourishment, exercise, and development that applies to your super-natural level of life as much as it does to the natural level. Your spirit is nourished by knowledge, and by reflection and meditation on that knowledge. It is exercised by the application of your knowledge to life's daily situations. Through this exercise and God's continued assistance, your spirit grows in its appreciation of truth, goodness, and beauty, and in its desire and ability to live by its principles and ideals.

10 Even the man who desires to achieve a purely natural development of his spiritual powers, i.e., his intellectual and moral powers, must follow the above procedure of nourish-ment, exercise, and growth. For instance, it requires years of study and experience to become an expert teacher, lawyer, doctor, etc. Yet, some of these same people fail to develop their supernatural spiritual powers beyond their childhood training. They are emotionally unable to strive without seeing visible, quick, or perfect results, or unwilling to work without feeling some sensible satis-

faction or gaining some earthly advantage. Though their professional knowledge and experience may place them above others in one area they are inferior to others in the matter of living within a religious frame of reference, i.e., by seeing God as the center of their being.

11   A number of people are confused or upset by the conflicts they experience or imagine between their natural needs, wants, and habits, and the requirements of their religious commitment. They do not realize that such conflicts are quite "normal" to mortal man in this life. Jesus experienced conflicting emotions within Himself on a number of occasions, e.g., after his fast in the desert, (Matt. 4:1-22), and in His agonizing prayer in the garden of Gethsemane. (Matt. 26:36-46) Just as He was subjected to some conflicting needs, wants, and emotions on these occasions so is every man subjected to the same experience at one time or another. Your problem becomes one of seeing some of these conflicts as "normal" in view of your life history or the nature of the situation at hand. On the other hand you must be realistic and honest enough to realize that some of your conflicts are due to your own

disorderly needs, wants, or emotional habits. When these latter conflicts occur, you owe it to yourself, to those around you, and to God to work at the diminution or elimination of the disorderly elements. On a number of occasions, you will have to realize that internal and external conflicts are not entirely incompatible with your supernatural state of union with God. They arise from the very nature of man. Consider the following facts of life. They are the broad facts that must be included in the life of most people.

12 As a new-born infant, you were welcomed into this world by a number of people who were involved with you in one way or another. For some time, during your infancy, your evident helplessness impelled your elders to attend to your every need. As you grew through and out of infancy, your bodily and emotional strengths and weaknesses, together with your inner dispositions, made you an easy, average, or difficult charge. The physical burdens, emotional concerns, social involvements and economic situation of your parents also influenced the manner in which they took care of you. Their love for you was limited by these and any other particular factors that played a part in their personal

lives. In other words, they could do just so much for you and no more. They could satisfy your needs and wants only in proportion to their own needs, wants, strengths and limitations.

13 Eventually your elders began the long training period which is the experience of every child and adolescent. With the dedication and limitations of their individual natures, they applied themselves to the task of conditioning you in the attitudes and habits which they considered necessary for your development into a successful adult. Between your first lessons in basic personal habits and the last stages of your intellectual, moral, and religious formation, you were guided, controlled, curbed, and compelled along the channels that produced your present personality, i.e., the sum total of particular qualities and traits which mark you as the distinct kind of individual you turned out to be.

14 Your life as an infant, child, and adolescent was a mixture of satisfactions and frustrations. Your elders and tutors could not always permit you to follow your spontaneous feelings, unharnessed emotions, and unenlightened desires. On many occasions, their

expectations and demands clashed with your wants and inclinations. Since you depended so utterly on their approval, acceptance and support, you often had to comply with the requirements of your elders in spite of your contrary feelings, needs and desires. Your dependency aroused too much anxiety for you to resist their wishes as much as you would have liked to. Thus, torn between your need to adjust to your elders and tutors, and your need to achieve some degree of self-expression and self-defense, you gradually developed the personal habits by which you live at present.

15 Had your parents and tutors been the wisest of people, they would still have been obliged to counteract your early-life urges and inclinations on many occasions. Without a solid formation of good natural habits, your later moral and religious training would have been extremely difficult, if not impossible. However, being human your elders had their own personal history with its limitations and shortcomings. They had their own individual views about the kind of person you "should be" and their own idea as to how you should achieve this goal. They taught and trained you not only with the knowledge and experi-

ence which they had acquired, but also with the particular prejudices, preferences, mistaken notions and emotional attitudes by which they applied their knowledge and experience to everyday life.

16 In so far as you found the authority and guidance of your parents reasonable, you were inclined to fulfill their wishes and requirements willingly. In so far as you felt that their demands were unreasonable or too difficult, you were inclined to ease the strain as best you could. Thus, you were sometimes caught between what you felt you "should do" and what you felt you could not achieve. At times this conflict inclined you to resent your parents, at least internally. This inclination aroused some sense of guilt or some measure of anxiety within you. Other authority figures affected you somewhat the same. Unconsciously, you may even have directed some of your resentment toward parents against other authority figures, e.g., teachers, religious leaders, police, or certain domineering adults. This tendency to express one's resentments toward some scapegoat, accounts in part for the negative attitudes of teenagers against adults in general. This phase of life persists in some people long after they have outgrown their teenage inadequacy, insecurity and anxiety. They continue to face life's daily situations with more emotion than the situation requires.

17   Another external source of conflict in your early life, was your involvement with other children, both at home and outside the family circle. Rivalry and competition among children is a common experience. Adults do not always appreciate how much this early interpersonal experience may affect the emotional development of the children involved in it. Your expanding needs and evolving wants often conflicted with the needs and wants of your peers. Your playmates, classmates, and junior acquaintances represented a world that threatened your sense of well-being in a thousand ways. Your efforts at self-defense were challenged time and again. The habits you had developed thus far were partly strengthened and partly modified as you tried to adjust to this world where imagination and emotions were sometimes more convincing than the world of grownups. The conflicts facing you on this level played a strong part in the further development of your growing personality.

18   Another source of conflict in your forma-

tive years, was your personal experience with
the moral views and religious beliefs of your
parents and elders. Your image of God came
less from how they described Him than from
their personal behavior toward you when you
misbehaved. Their actions and attitudes
toward you were something of "how God must
feel about you" in these situations. Though
you may have tried to believe in God's
fatherly understanding and personal love,
your emotional response to God and religion
depends to some extent on those adults who
played a central role in your religious training.
True, God has exercised His supernatural
influence on you through the years, but his
divine assistance is not intended to erase
automatically the emotional impressions of
early life. With God's help, you are to build
up a supernatural vision and strength that
will counterbalance this natural impression
that still makes itself felt from time to time.
In your daily effort to live by God's supernatural gifts of faith, hope and charity, you
are taking personal command of your daily
fight against the unreasoning emotional habits
that seek to rule over your self-management.

19   Thus, you see, how your past and present
life are united as a branch is joined to its

trunk. The conflicts you face today are more than the mere external situations which develop from present circumstances. These conflicts are composed of the present circumstances plus the needs, wants, and the mental and emotional habits with which you and those involved view these circumstances. The attitudes and outlook with which you and these other people view the present situation, are a complex development that took root in your early life experiences and branched out through the subsequent years. Though you have forgotten the vast majority of these individual experiences, they leave their mark on your present characteristic approach to life's daily problems. In short, the attitudes and outlook which developed during your formative years, are so intertwined with your present thinking and feelings, that they continue to influence your highest aspirations and noblest effort in some way. This is also true of the people with whom you must deal this day. In proportion as you can see yourself and them in this perspective, you will face your inner conflicts and interpersonal difficulties with greater understanding and readiness to make due allowance for the needs and habits that are disturbing you and those with whom you deal.

20　On the other hand, it will always be within your power to strive for an adult desire to face facts, accept truth, and practice daily toward a more objective self-management. However, you must be fully aware that even with God's help, it will take time to modify or change attitudes and habits which took years to develop into their present structure and strength. Your greatest achievement may well consist in this: that you were willing to keep practicing without undue disappointment in failure and without unreasonable strain in the face of strongly entrenched attitudes and habits. For some people, "just trying" may be the only proof they can ever give of their love of truth and justice. For others, "trying" is not enough. They want "results," visible, tangible results. If they can take the time, work for the necessary knowledge and understanding, and continue their daily effort to practice what they have learned, they will eventually achieve whatever results lie within their capabilities. Having done what they could, they ought to accept realistically the limitations of their efforts. No man can do more than that. God Himself requires no more than that.

16

Man's Daily Struggle For Self-Possession

1 THE preceding chapter may seem to be blaming others for your shortcomings. It may appear to make you altogether too innocent of defects for which you may consider yourself accountable. If these are your present sentiments, you have misunderstood the message of the preceding chapter. That message is only a small portion of a larger and more complex message, namely, the story of your formation as a human person, and of your development into the specific personality you now possess.

2 There is no question of blame or accusation, whether of yourself or anyone else. It is simply a matter of gathering whatever facts will help you understand yourself a little better, so that you may gradually develop a more realistic self-realization in daily life. Since self-doubts or self-rejection make self-realization almost impossible, you owe it to yourself, and therefore to God, to strive for whatever knowledge and understanding you can achieve. Self-knowledge is often difficult to attain because of strong emotional obstacles or unconscious mental blocks. In your

efforts at self-reorganization, you need to understand your nature as fully as possible. Your nature repeats itself many times each day in your personal habits of body, mind and spirit. For this reason, you need to reflect often on the basic facts and fundamental principles of your human behavior, with a view to absorbing them gradually into your innermost attitudes and outlook on life. As the old teaching principle states it: "Repetition is the mother of learning." It is also the root of self-understanding and self-reorganization.

3 Basically, all men are alike in this respect: Human nature has a primary drive to self-fulfillment. Every man feels fulfilled in so far as he can satisfy his felt needs and wants. Only in this way, can he achieve, maintain, or defend his sense of well-being. This sense of well-being is the goal of all your efforts at self-fulfillment, whether conscious or unconscious, whther direct or indirect. As long as you enjoy a sense of well-being, you will feel that life is worth living. Your nature will resist or escape anything threatening or frustrating her sense of well-being. This much all men have in common. In this respect, all men are alike.

4   At the same time, no two people are exactly alike. Apart from the basic needs and wants, common to all men, you also have your very particular needs, individual wants, and personal feelings. These developed in their own way through your past experiences, especially in the early, formative years. They continue to exert some influence on every habit of yours, and they play some part, be it ever so indirect, in everything you imagine, think, say or do today. All of your needs and wants, whether of body, mind or spirit, are so interrelated, so balanced and counter-balanced, so interspersed and intertwined, as to make you the unique individual you are today. In all God's creation, there never was and never will be another person exactly like you. Therefore, in your daily efforts to achieve, maintain or protect your sense of well-being, you have your own particular patterns of self-expression, self-satisfaction, and self-defense. In this, no two men are exactly alike.

5   Man is a mysterious combination of matter, mind and spirit. He inherits a complex biological organism, namely, his body, which plays a mysterious part in the development of his personality. Just how much your bodily

organs and functions affect your mental, emotional, intellectual and moral powers, is far from settled by the experts. Moreover, there is still much to learn about how man's mental, emotional and spiritual operations can cause psychosomatic ailments in his body. Well may you wonder, "Where does the body end and the soul begin in man's life-processes of body, mind and spirit?"

6 And yet, no matter how deep and intricate the mystery of human nature may be, you are not entirely ignorant of it. As you consider your personal habits and experience, you can recall how you sometimes feel sorry for yourself, sometimes proud of yourself, and sometimes disgusted or angry at yourself. In other words, you are *for* yourself at one time and *against* yourself at another. Within reasonable limits, this is a normal, human experience. On occasion, however, it can be a downright disadvantage, or even injustice, against you or those with whom you deal.

7 In proportion as you achieve self-possession, you can become your own master, i.e., you can manage your daily behavior with enlightened judgment and spontaneous choice. The self-possessed person is "at home with himself." He has learned to respect his own

talents, experience, preferences, achievements, and state in life. He understands his "feelings" but will not always allow them to do his thinking for him. He follows them when they make sense, i.e., when they agree with the facts. He is a man of confidence, whether it be confidence from some natural source, or supernatural confidence in God. Thus he is generally composed, in control of his faculties, and in command of his behavior, whether in company or alone. This description may seem rather discouraging to you, as you recall your human deficiencies and shortcomings. And yet, you need not surrender to discouragement.

8 Whatever your present degree of self-possession and self-management, you can, with the proper attitude, advance toward this desirable goal each hour of every day. You will not make great, noticeable, consistent strides with each effort, nor will you eventually arrive at perfection itself. But then, neither God nor reasonable people expect perfection of you. All that anyone can expect of you is that you do what you can to grow in self-knowledge, self-understanding, self-acceptance, and self-management, with due respect for your nature's pace and limitations.

9 Though you may be eager to begin a campaign toward a fuller self-possession, you can succeed only in so far as you are disposed to build your life on reality and truth. Unfortunately, reality and truth are not always easy to attain. They are often obscured or distorted by emotions arising in you or in those with whom you deal. Human nature's strongest drive is her drive to protect herself from the unpleasant. What is pleasant or unpleasant, is not always decided by objective facts. It is often decided by "how you feel about the facts." No matter how convinced you may be in your clear intellectual view of things, you can still be swayed by your emotional attitudes in any situation.

10 How you see reality today, depends on how you were taught to view it in your formative years, not only by words, but especially by example. How you understand the truth at present, depends on how it was colored, slanted, stressed, and applied by your childhood elders, tutors, and associates. In varying degrees, your present mental attitudes and moral habits are deeply connected with your past emotional experiences. These experiences have left their imprint on your nervous system, mind, and spirit to this very

day. The challenge of earthly life is simply this: Are you willing to try each day, to let your "thinking" be guided by reality and truth rather than by your unrealistic "feelings" in the matter? In proportion as you achieve this "scientific" attitude toward life, you will grow toward the integrity and peace of the self-possessed man.

11 From the moment you seriously consider facing life with a realistic outlook, your old emotional habits will present a variety of obstacles to your new effort. In spite of your evident good will and sincere endeavors, you will still respond to conflicts more spontaneously in your old, undesired ways than with your new, desired attitudes. You will find yourself behaving like a person who really wants a painful tooth extracted, but cannot help pulling away from the dentist's helping hand. This need not surprise nor discourage you. Your present life, with all its good intentions and intelligent efforts, is like a new branch growing out of the original trunk of your earthly life. You cannot prevent some of your old feelings, ideas, and tendencies from entering into your new attitudes and efforts. On the other hand, your new thinking and practices will gradually direct your de-

sires and efforts toward more realistic goals.
12   Crying over spilt milk is a waste of precious time. It is far wiser to take up where you find yourself along the road of life, and to proceed toward whatever growth and dvelopment are still possible to you. If you need divine assurance in your efforts, read and reflect on Christ's parable on the laborers in the vineyard (Matt. 20:1-16), the parable on the talents (Matt. 25:14-30), and the parable about the widow's mite (Mark 12:41-44). God asks no more of any man than he is able to achieve in his present circumstances. Moreover, it doesn't matter what others may think or say about you, only God can gauge your true worth and merits. Live each day as it comes. Do not spend a second bemoaning the mistakes of yesterday. Refuse to waste any of today's energies on needless worry about possible problems that may arise tomorrow. Your best proof of sorrow for past mistakes for faults, and your best preparation for future difficulties and hardships, is in this simple formula: Learn from your mistakes and apply what you learn to future situations. You will then be living each today as best you can with the help of God and whomever else you may need. God asks no more of you

than that, and your fellowmen have no right
to expect more.

17
Self-Satisfaction
Versus Fear of Punishment

¹MUCH as you may wish to achieve fulfillment in your earthly life, you will
still have to contend with opposing forces
within yourself. Do not be surprised if you
feel little or no interest in working for a fuller
self-possession and a more balanced self-
management in daily life. The project may
seem too difficult because of your established
habits, or too hopeless because of past
failures. Then again, you may feel some
apprehension about other people's reactions
to your new effort. Every man sees life within
his own frame of reference, i.e., he sees and
judges people and things in the light of his
own needs, wants and interests. For this
reason, some people may project their own
feelings onto your behavior. This possibility
can arouse some measure of insecurity,
anxiety, or unwanted hostility within you.
2 No one can really blame you for feeling
this way. You have had a long experience

with your own unpleasant emotional habits, as well as with the disturbing habits of others. Even in your early years of life, you found yourself compelled to consider how others might feel about your efforts toward self-satisfaction. In your formative years, your parents and tutors felt their responsibility in your training. Some form of discipline was a necessary part of this training. Since you could not help living on your feelings and emotions, your elders had to create contrary feelings and emotions within you. They did this by presenting you with the prospect of punishment for your misbehavior.

3 Punishment means different things to different people. What it means to each individual, depends on how he experienced it in early life. It may have been administered in the spirit of a personal retaliation, a sort of tit-for-tat; or in the spirit of an objective retribution, like a rebalancing of the scales of justice; or finally as a positive act of constructive discipline, to help the offender see the advantages of orderly behavior. No matter how your punishers meant it, your view of punishment in your early life depended also on how you felt it emotionally. In those years of utter dependence on others, you needed

to feel sure that those on whom you depended really meant you no harm, even in the act of punishment. In proportion as you felt somehow resented, disapproved, or threatened for being the person you are, punishment brought you more than the objective impressions mentioned above. It also brought you some measure of basic insecurity, i.e., a feeling of inner helplessness.

4   Having experienced your personal limitations so often in early life, you cannot help feeling somewhat insecure in your dealings with others. Though your self-confidence has developed with time and experience, your early self-doubts have left some lasting impressions. Today your behavior with others depends more on how you feel about your ability to deal with them, rather than on how they behave toward you. In other words, the more self-confident you feel about yourself, the more easily are you able to see and treat others as they really are.

5   You have a natural right to satisfy your personal needs and wants, as far as this is possible and permissible in your present circumstances. As long as you violate no reasonable law of man or commandment of God, you are not forbidden to enjoy a sense of

well-being in your daily life. The opinions, judgments, and preferences of others need not disturb you too much, since you alone know your personal problems and needs. Even Jesus was subjected to the criticism and punishment of others for daring to act contrary to their expectations. At the same time, He did not do so with childish emotional attitudes, but with an intelligent, purposeful desire to fulfill His mission on earth.

6 You too have a mission on earth, namely to live in accordance with your daily needs, wants, duties, and supernatural inspirations. In your daily efforts to achieve self-satisfaction, your problem will be one of maintaining a balance between your unreasoning, emotional tendencies, your intelligent, grace-inspired self-fulfillment, and the genuine needs and rights of others. The more you understand that others came by their frame of reference just as you did, the more easily will you be able to let them be themselves without taking them more seriously than they deserve. Like you, they had their early experiences, misunderstandings, and emotional self-defenses. In their very act of "punishing" you with their retaliation or retribution, they may be just as sincere as you are. In your

efforts to defend yourself, beware of attributing to them more malice than they actually have. Like you, they are often victims of their own inner needs, wants, tensions and emotions.

7 The more you see others within this frame of reference, the more will you be inclined to tolerate their rigid disturbing habits and fixed annoying mannerisms. On the other hand, the more you concentrate on your own feelings and emotions, so much the more will you be inclined to withdraw from others timidly, or strike back at them resentfully for the inconvenience or annoyance they cause you. God does not want you to surrender your natural right to seek your own satisfaction and fulfillment. On the other hand, a mature religious person does not feel cheated or exploited when giving of himself for the sake of others. In his larger vision of life, he sees his self-giving as a privileged opportunity to imitate the Heavenly Father in creation, the Divine Son in redemption, and the Holy Spirit in His constant work of raising men's hearts to the better things in life.

8 With this divine vision, you will not easily surrender to any vague "fear of punishment" from God or man. You will not submit to undue shame over your limitations, un-reasoning self-blame for the shortcomings you see within yourself, or needless urges to "make reparation" for unintended failures. Your peace will proceed from your trust in God's fatherly understanding and Christ's self-sacrifice, more than from your own visible personal achievements. Let your fear be "realistic," i.e., based on objective facts rather than on your fantasies or feelings about the facts. This is the fear of the wise, not the fear of the childish mind or the cowardly heart. In all your dealings with others, let reality and truth be your guide. If God is for you, who can really hurt you? Jesus has told you in a number of ways that God is for you as long as you are intelligently for yourself, i.e., by seeking your self-satisfaction and self-fulfillment within the real possibilities and legitimate opportunities at your disposal this day.

18
The Real Self Versus the Self-Ideal

1   AT ONE time or another, every human being experiences some doubts about his personal worth or his daily performance.

Do not be surprised, annoyed or uneasy when this occurs. You cannot always be sure "what you should be" or "how you should behave" in particular situations. As the sky is constantly changing with the moving atmosphere and shifting sunbeams, man's attitudes are constantly being affected by his ever-changing circumstances and passing moods. In a sense, you are not quite the same person, as you live through the various experiences of one single day. Each hour brings its particular situation, and each situation has its particular effect on your disposition and outlook.

2   Much as you may yearn for a well-ordered constancy in your daily behavior or performance, you will often fall short of your desired ideal. In spite of good intentions and sincere efforts at self-improvement, you cannot achieve more than a limited self-control and an imperfect self-management. And even that achievement would fall shorter still, but for the grace of God. Though these words may seem pessimistic, they are not intended, nor transmitted, in that spirit. The true optimist, is not one who sees more than reality offers, but one who seeks to make the most of what reality does offer him. You do yourself

an injustice in blaming yourself blindly when your non-voluntary urges, feelings, or emotions move you to behave against your better judgment. Your emotional maturity and moral formation may be gauged most reliably by 1) your readiness to understand your emotional regressions, 2) your willingness to learn from your moral weaknesses, 3) your practical preparations against future recurrences of undesirable habits, and 4) a determined resolve to keep trying, regardless of the failures. The wise man is not one who never errs, but one who never stops learning from his errors.

3 Some people are reluctant to spend time in self-study. Their argument for this reluctance might run somewhat as follows: "Why waste precious time and energy in self-centered study? Is it not healthier to foster mental, emotional, and spiritual growth by reaching out to God through religious knowledge and prayer and by helping my fellow-man with more positive attitudes and more generous efforts to make this world a better place for others?"

4 These people seem to see self-study as a soul-shriveling activity which distracts one from the larger needs of the community. Nothing could be farther from the truth. A

realistic self-study leads not only to self-understanding, but also to a broader understanding and deeper appreciation of human nature in general. It disposes you to accept yourself as you really are, rather than live under an emotional cloud of indiscriminate self-doubts, unwarranted self-contempt, or unjustified guilt feelings. This honest self-acceptance does not diminish your desire to improve with experience. It simply takes all undue anxiety and unrealistic expectations out of your daily efforts. You are better able to see your limitations and shortcomings as "natural and normal," rather than a cause for shame. You can look on your pesonal talents and opportunities as your daily path to self-fulfillment and personal concern for the fulfillment of others.

5 How you feel about yourself affects your relationship with both God and your fellow-men. When your self-esteem is marred by a negative self-image, you can neither give generously to others nor receive gratefully from them. Your self-giving will be hampered by doubts about your personal worth, and your gratitude will be hindered by a sense of not deserving consideration or kindness. Though you may not understand why, you

will feel that you have little to give, and not much to claim or expect. Self-knowledge may stir up negative feelings at first, but in the long run, self-understanding will bring greater peace and joy. A persevering effort at self-understanding will eventually help you see yourself a little more through God's eyes. In His fatherly view of your daily behavior, God takes into consideration all the forces, influences and limitations that affect your daily self-management. Though you will always have some measure of self-doubt, you can also develop a stronger faith in your own sincerity and a deeper confidence that God is really as fatherly as Jesus described Him in His parable of the prodigal son. (Luke 15:11-32)

6 Every human being has some kind of self-ideal, i.e., some image of the kind of person he would like to be or intends to be. Though this self-ideal is not always fully conscious or thoroughly clear, it plays a strong part in your everyday behavior. In proportion as your self-ideal is realistic, balanced, and satisfying, it is a valid source of inspiration to you, and a constructive guide toward self-fulfillment. It inclines you to be reasonably content with yourself, and dis-

poses you to be intelligently considerate of others in their difficult moods or behavior. It even inclines you to turn easily and confidently to God in time of physical tensions, emotional stress and mental turmoil.

7   When, however, your self-ideal represents what you "must" be in order to satisfy your sense of inadequacy, insecurity and anxiety, it becomes a cruel, merciless goal which must be reached regardless of the price to yourself or others. Your anxiety cannot be allayed by anything but a perfect performance modeled on this perfectionistic self-ideal. Anything short of perfection arouses self-doubts, guilt feelings, strained efforts, or sheer discouragement. Though the victims of this unrealistic, unreasonable self-ideal, do not realize it, they may not regain their sense of well-being even when they do achieve a perfect performance. Why not? Because the sense of well-being can also be disrupted by the exhausting efforts required by the anxiety-dominated performance. Thus, these victims are caught between their compulsive need to satisfy their self-ideal, and their conflicting need to consider their nature's most basic primary needs and God-given limitations.

8   How does a person become so unreason-

able toward himself? What makes him violate his primary drive to self-fulfillment even when it becomes a matter of self-preservation? The whole process seems to be against nature. Though many people know that they are perfectionistic in their tendencies, few consider their perfectionistic trends extreme. Most perfectionists see their perfectionism as a gift, a virtue, or a sheer necessity in their case. In reality, it is often none of these. The realistic perfectionist accepts the real limitations of the realities with which he deals. He does not necessarily like them, but he accepts them as part of his life on earth.

9   Once again, a brief review of your history will help put the matter into its true perspective. Your present self-image, i.e., "How you see yourself" grew out of your life-experience. As a child, you learned to see yourself through the eyes of the adults in charge of your early training, schooling, and moral development. Through them you learned what kind of person you "should be." Your sense of well-being depended on your fulfillment of their standards. On the other hand, it also depended on your satisfying some of your own needs and wants. Thus, your early efforts at fulfillment, were a struggle between your

spontaneous needs and the expectations of others. Your self-image, i.e., "the kind of person you felt you were," was considered good or bad, according as it did or did not agree with the requirements of your elders. With advancing age and experience, your needs multiplied in number and grew in complexity. Your developing nature craved a broader self-fulfillment. You found it increasingly difficult to fulfill the self-ideal of your earlier years. You needed to be more self-reliant. You craved a greater freedom to express your own feelings, follow more of your own desires, and pattern your behavior more closely to your evolving feelings, ideas and ideals. Though your present thinking capacity has grown with time and experience, the emotional habits of those formative years continue to influence your present-day thought processes. Even in your exercise of supernatural faith, your natural emotional habits still play a significant part. For better or worse they affect your attitudes toward God, morality and eternity.

10 However complex your outlook on life may now be, its main emotional bent was fashioned in childhood. On the other hand, your present self-ideal no longer represents simply "what you need to be in order to please others." Your fulfillment and sense of well-being now depends on a larger variety of needs and wants. Your present self-ideal is now a complexus of 1) a modified compliance with early training, 2) a limited adaptation to later learning and experience, and 3) a mixed response to the natural behavior of people and the supernatural urgings of God's graces.

11 In proportion as you can absorb the message of this chapter, your daily life can, with the help of God's grace, become a daily balanced achievement of mental, emotional, and spiritual growth. In its original strivings human nature is constantly drawn toward reality, facts, and truth. Man goes to extremes through ignorance, misunderstanding, intolerable pressures and moral weakness. Just where human limitations end and malice begins, is often a mystery to the offender himself. For this reason, you will always have some measure of self-doubts and some need of supernatural hope in God's fatherly understanding and forgiveness.

12 When you feel that life's daily combat is too difficult, you may well need to consider whether the difficulties are not being magnified, intensified or multiplied by your unreasoning natural feelings of inadequacy, insecurity, and anxiety. Is it not possible that your early emotional formation is unbalancing your later intellectual and religious development? May it not be that your self-ideal is beyond all reasonable efforts, and that you are measuring yourself by its impossible standards? If you are doing this, how can you avoid despising your self-image and judging yourself guilty?

13 As your wisdom grows, you will become better acquainted with the "real you," i.e., the "full you." You are the sum total of everything you feel, imagine, think, need, desire, say, do and omit. Your nature is the work of God. It is constantly reaching out for its fulfillment and defense, in body, mind and spirit. Under the stress of your inborn drives, acquired needs and developed habits, your self-evaluation is often confused by your conflicting notions and emotions, and your self-management is often weakened by your contrary inclinations. Amid this inner stress and interpersonal strains, you may tend to doubt your adequacy to deal with life, or fear for your security with God or people.

14 Jesus presented a supernatural counterbalance to this inner division of your nature.

God created you for fulfillment, not only in eternity, but also in this earthly life. He speaks to you not only through supernatural revelation, but also through your nature's basic demand for an intelligent self-concern and an orderly self-fulfillment. God expects you to help yourself in so far as you can, and to depend on His fatherly providence in so far as you must. Jesus was considered a rebel against the religious establishment of His time, because He insisted that no law could rightly disregard man's basic natural needs. For this reason, He allowed His disciples to pick and eat corn on the Sabbath (Matt. 12:1-8), cured a number of sick people on the Sabbath (John 9:14-16), and publicly disagreed with some of the temple laws that disregarded the rights of parents to the support of their children (Matt. 15:1-9). His message on these occasions may be summed up thus: "God is not only just, not only merciful, but also and primarily reasonable." The more you appreciate this broader view of God, the more will you strive for an intelligent, realistic, balanced self-fulfillment.

19

Achievement Versus Fear of Failure

1 A NUMBER of people go through life dissatisfied with their occupation, unhappy about their social status, or anxious about some threat to their physical, psychological, or moral well-being. Others are constantly dissatisfied with their lost opportunities or with their past life in general. Occasionally all of these people feel some desire to do something about their particular situation. They may even make an initial effort toward achieving a solution. Too often, however, this effort gradually wanes and fades away. A sense of hopelessness seeps imperceptibly into the original desire for achievement, and gradually dissipates the initial inspiration and enthusiasm. This hoplessness may be hidden under the guise of disinterest or a change of mind, but basically it is a sense of not being able to perform as one would like. Hopelessness, in its numberless disguises and countless degrees of intensity, stems from several sources within human nature itself. Perhaps the most common source is "fear of failure." Its victim may not even suspect the real reason for his discour-

agement and surrender. He may only be aware of one or several superficial reasons. Unless he understands the true nature of his problem, he cannot help himself or others with the same problem.

2 Every man has some measure of this conflict between achievement and fear of failure. The realistic person tries to keep his efforts within the bounds of his known capacity and proven limitation. When he undertakes a doubtful achievement, he makes allowance for his doubts and for possible failure. When disappointed at his poor showing, he tries to learn whether or how he may improve. When, however, he has good reason to admit his inadequacy or limitations in some particular achievement, he tries to face the fact and to live with it as best he can. He may not exactly like the fact, but he knows that there is more to his life than just this particular matter.

3 The immature person, on the contrary, tends to go to extremes. He may demand of himself a perfect performance, without even considering the possibility or acceptability of any lesser results. Then again, he may be so unsure of his ability to succeed, as to profess disinterest in the achievement. Consciously or unconsciously, he may fear his inner shame at falling short of his self-ideal. Or again, he may dread a possible humiliation by what others may think or say about his achievement. Though he may deny the fact, he actually considers any result short of perfection as a "failure." And why? Because only perfect results can forestall any self-disgust or guilt-feelings, and prevent any criticism, or humiliation from others. In either case, he is emotionally immobilized between his desire to achieve and his equally strong fear of possible failure. Most people consider themselves free of this conflict, because they look at it in its extreme manifestations. However, this conflict occurs quite often in milder forms and lesser intensity. Therefore, it would be wise of you to study it more fully, so as to achieve a greater inner peace and interpersonal harmony when friction arises from this source.

4   As you look at this conflict in perspective, you will find it more interesting than disturbing. It is a development from man's formative years. In that stage of life, you were inclined to follow your feelings spontaneously and to satisfy your needs and wants without consideration for others. Your parents, teachers,

and others often had occasion to correct or punish you for what you said or did. Their attitudes and expectations influenced your thinking more than you realized at the time. From them you got your initial ideas of the kind of person you "should be" or "must be." Their acceptance and approval played a major part in the formation and stability of your sense of well-being. Consequently, you felt a strong need to fulfill their expectations and demands. Only in this way could you maintain your sense of well-being.

5 Like most people, you may feel quite certain that you have completely outgrown your childhood needs and wants. Some of those needs, however, are basic. They will be with you to your dying day. Their immediate goals and methods of expression have changed with your age, experience, and state in life, but their primary goal remains what it was from the beginning, i.e., to maintain and protect your sense of well-being. Whether you be young, middle-aged, or old, your primary need is the preservation of your sense of well-being through the fulfillment of your present needs and wants. Therefore you cannot escape some measure of conflict between possible achievement and fear of failure.

Each time you fail in self-fulfillment, you suffer some degree of insecurity, anxiety, or anger, i.e., your sense of well-being is disturbed.

6 Since you are a social being by your very nature, you must depend on others for the fulfillment of some of your needs and wants. Your fulfillment cannot always be assured either in what you want or how you want it. You are limited not only by your own personal nature, but also by the needs and wants of others. No two people are identical. They do not have the same number, quality, or combination of needs and wants. Though you may not see the differences between others and yourself, the differences are there. So many physical, mental, emotional, spiritual, and supernatural elements enter into any one achievement, that no two people can perform it with perfect equality. To compare yourself with others, is a sheer waste of precious time and energy. You are too individual a being to be compared with anyone. True, you may strive to imitate the admirable qualities and achievements of another person, but the two performances will always have their own distinctive differences and merits. One who fails in a competitive venture, may actually

have performed with far greater courage or perseverance than the victor, in view of their particular natural gifts and supernatural graces. Only God is in a position to judge the relative merits of the two. As for people's estimate of you, their judgments are usually modified or blocked by their own past history and present emotional involvements.

7 You are in no position to label yourself a failure in any achievement unless you can validly accuse yourself of malice, i.e., a willfully bad attitude, disposition, or intention. Even when you do so accuse yourself, you are often too emotionally involved to achieve a truly objective self-estimate. In working toward a deeper self-understanding and a fuller self-management, be reasonable in your efforts and grateful for the outcome. Be it great or small, it is your achievement. It is your personal addition to God's work of creation. As He left His divine fingerprints on His works, so do you leave your mark on this world with each reasonable thought, word, desire, or effort. If you feel that your efforts and achievements are too insignificant to bring glory to God, reflect on what Jesus said of His heavenly Father. God not only created the tiniest birds of the air, but He is also concerned

about the well-being of each one. (Matt. 6:26)

8 On the eve of His death, Jesus underwent a soul-wrenching agony in the olive grove at Gethsemane. Even as He was contending with His own human conflict, He looked on His sleeping disciples with the words: "The Spirit is willing, but the flesh is weak." (Matt. 26:41) He was not making a sentimental excuse for them, but simply stating a fact. You must often remind yourself that you are human, and therefore limited by your very nature. Much as you may hate to be reminded of this fact, it remains a fact. You may turn your attention from it, or strive to disregard it by undertaking achievements beyond your energies, talents, or graces. Nevertheless, each time you overstep the natural or supernatural boundaries of your personal nature, you will face "failure," not necessarily a culpable failure, but a failure that is usually natural and normal to you.

9 Your maturity lies in being able to live within the realities that God has placed at your disposal. You do have some talents. There are a number of achievements which are definitely within your powers. Some achievements will require more application than others. You will not always be able to judge whether you have done your "best," but then God does not require this of you. He asks only that you perform your daily duties with a reasonable attention and a realistic attitude. When one achievement is over, you may turn to the next, or you may relax until you are able, or intelligently disposed, to take up your next activity.

10 Beware of morbid introspection! In your desire for a flawless perfection, you may be tempted to study everything you think, feel, say, or do, ever looking for possible defects, or criticizing yourself for not having behaved "better" than you did. The defects and faults which require your proper concern, will usually come to your attention through the negative response of people who are not habitually difficult or overly sensitive, or through your own observations in your calmer and more realistic moments. Vague, indefinite "possible failures" are not worth bothering with. There will always be some self-doubt about something or other in the mind of the average man. This is the normal state of human nature on earth. The true "adult" understands this fact, and learns to go about his daily routine with an intelligent disregard of his indefinable fear of failure.

20

Independence Versus the Need to Belong

1 LIVING in society requires a certain amount of conformity and self-restraint. You learned this from your earliest childhood. For years you had to depend on your elders and contend with your equals. You often had to disregard your spontaneous feelings and control your deepest desires, in order to avoid arousing others against you. This is the experience of every human being during his formative years. Consequently, the average child and youth indulges in many a daydream about his ultimate emancipation from the domination of others and his freedom to live life as he wishes.

2 This desire for independence is quite normal. It proceeds from your very nature as an individual human being. Every man has his particular needs and wants, his personal likes and dislikes, and his established preferences and prejudices. Because of this fact, you cannot avoid an occasional disagreement or contention with others. No matter how complex the interpersonal situation may be, or how simple the motivation of the conflicting persons may seem, their clashes are ultimately

due to the need which each one has to maintain, defend, or restore his own sense of well-being. They are both striving to prevent their own feelings of inadequacy, insecurity, anxiety, or anger from upsetting them. Since any form of interpersonal doubts, threats or aggression is capable of arousing one or other of the above-mentioned feelings, a number of people try to eliminate these situations through independence.

3 This desire for independence can be both normal and healthy. However, independence must be rightly understood and wisely asserted if you are to achieve an intelligent self-management and a realistic self-fulfillment. Independence does not mean "doing as you please" without due regard for the legitimate rights and justified feelings of others. Neither does it mean "putting others in their place," simply because you feel that they are taking advantage of you in some way. Even when you are permitted, or even required, to defend your sense of well-being from the unwarranted behavior of others, you are not to do it like a child acting on blind feelings or unreasoning emotions. Your nature requires you to act as an adult and assert your independence with a sense of responsibility. You owe it

to yourself and your neighbor, to give fair consideration to his feelings and views and to make due allowance for his emotional, intellectual, and moral limitations in each situation.

4   Above all, your independence does not mean "not needing anybody for anything." Man is a social being by his very nature. In His work of creation, God said, "It is not good that man should be alone. I will make him a helpmate." (Gen. 2:18) Every man needs to communicate and cooperate with his fellow-men in some kind of family relationship, friendship, or community participation. Every individual has some need of being understood and accepted for what he is. He needs a certain amount of approval in his behavior to re-assure him in his moments of self-doubt, and to bolster his self-confidence with others. He needs some achievement to demonstrate his success as an individual. He also needs to receive some measure of good will to sustain his sense of belonging to the various persons and groups on whom he depends in some way. True, you cannot depend solely and entirely on others for your inner sense of value, but their moral and emotional support does play a considerable part in the formation, confirmation, and balanced

growth of your satisfactory self-image and self-esteem.

5   The more you reflect on your natural need of others, the more you will understand why your desire for independence must be realistic. Every man has a natural drive toward self-fulfilllment. Every individual wants freedom to be himself and to seek his personal satisfaction and contentment in daily life. Since man is a social being, he must achieve his fulfillment among his fellow-men. This means that your desire for independence must necessarily be limited by the legitimate needs and wants of those around you. Just as they have no right to demand that you subordinate your basic needs and wants to suit their convenience, you have no right to demand that they surrender indiscriminately to your preferences and prejudices. The independence of each individual is limited by the equal independence of everyone else, and no individual can reasonably prefer his personal satisfaction to the common welfare of his community.

6   With this balanced view of life, you need not hesitate to strive for your personal independence within the laws of nature, society, and divine revelation. You have a God-given

right to be yourself, as long as you try to do so intelligently and reasonably. Though God made you into an image of Himself, your human nature is only a rough sketch of the divine nature. With the help of God's grace, your daily efforts to fulfill the requirements and needs of your daily routine, are constantly filling in your sketchy image of God. Each conscious moment of your daily life, lived in good will and divine grace, is an added contribution to your limited reflection of the divine goodness. On the other hand, in your most sincere endeavors to improve your earthly situation, do not expect to escape the basic problems of your human circumstances. Wherever you go, you bring your individual human nature with you. You still have your share of doubts, inadequacy, insecurity, fears, and tendencies to anger and hostility. Your neighbor also has his particular pattern of these same qualities.

7   Your personal sense of independence will grow in proportion as you develop an honest respect for yourself as a human being, in proportion as you learn to manage and control your needs and wants within the necessary limits of your nature and daily situations, and in proportion as you develop an intelligent

concern for the needs and wants of others. Much that is thought, said, or done by you and those around you, is conditioned by each one's past history and present emotional attitudes. The more constantly you are aware of this fact, the better disposed will you be to accept inevitable interpersonal friction with an intelligent resignation, an understanding tolerance of other people's weaknesses and defects, and a stubborn effort to make the best of life's daily situations.

8   The more you concentrate on your negative feelings and emotions, the more will you be limiting the good you might contribute to your own life and to the lives of others. Only with a positive attitude can you brighten your environment with a kind word, a friendly smile, or other gestures of good will. As for those who seem unable to accept you and your efforts, try to understand that their non-acceptance may well stem from emotional problems buried deep within them. Most people tend to interpret your behavior in the light of their own needs, wants, and emotional disposition of the moment. Since you cannot always remedy these situations, learn to live with them as far as you can by realizing that every man has his share of this problem.

9 In your efforts for independence, do not expect to achieve more than the limited independence of a realistic self-fulfillment. You cannot afford to alienate others altogether in your demand for unlimited independence. Every man needs some measure of communication with others. Solitary confinement can drive a man mad, as he reaches the end of his internal resources of mind and spirit. As plants must feed on the ground and atmosphere around them to sustain and fulfill their natural survival and growth, so does your nature seek her fulfillment through the people and things within her reach. Loneliness is one of man's most intolerable trials. You doom yourself to this in proportion as you disregard the needs and wants of others. Even if you tried to separate yourself from others through an intense union with God, you would still be limited by the particular graces which God may grant you. He may not want you to seclude yourself as much as you do. Most men are expected to give of themselves to the world around them, with due moderation and self-concern. How you make use of your natural and supernatural gifts, depends on your personal needs, wants, inclinations and opportunities. Within the limits

of your human nature and your measure of divine grace, you have some variety of choice in the use of your personal freedom. On the other hand, your self-determination is definitely limited by the laws of nature, grace and human society.

PART FOUR

Nature's Spontaneous Solutions

THOUGH every man would like to be in possession of his own feelings, imagination, thinking and decisions, he is often unable to achieve such possession. Like St. Paul, every man has his moments when he knows that he can do little more than "want" to think straight and "try" to behave in accordance with the objective facts of the present situation. His phantasies, emotions, and actions are sometimes beyond his control and management. At such times one can only assert his good will and believe in his own sincerity. This section will help the reader understand himself a little better, and thereby bring him a greater self-appreciation and a more reasonable self-acceptance.

21
Nature's Sensitivity to Stress

[1] TRY AS you may, you cannot resolve all problems, conflicts, and frustrations in your daily life. Your personal needs, wants, and drives are too numerous and complex for you to achieve a constant self-fulfillment. The same is true of the people with whom you must deal. Between your own inner needs, wants, problems, conflicts, and frustrations, and those of your fellow-men, it is simply inevitable that your sense of well-being should be disturbed from time to time. This is a fundamental condition of earthly human living, and you have to learn to live with it.

2   To get the most out of life, you need: 1) to work for whatever legitimate success and reasonable satisfaction you can achieve in your daily routine; 2) to face new challenges when necessary, rather than avoid them; 3) to deal with new situations realistically, i.e., make the most of them as far as circumstances will permit, without straining beyond your capacities; 4) to look upon your unintended failures and unexpected disappointments as a normal part of your daily experience; 5) to learn something constructive from

your mistakes and failures; and 6) to apply what you learned to your future experience.

3 This disposition to live life more fully, more daringly, and more realistically, will help you increase your frustration-tolerance. This tolerance will enable you to continue functioning in spite of your useless spontaneous resentments, disgust, discouragement, or anxieties. However, do not expect this to happen overnight. Only a patient, persevering practice in trial, error, and re-trial will bring you this desirable growth. Though a higher frustration-tolerance will not solve all your problems and conflicts, it will contribute to your future solutions by making you less sensitive to the ordinary stresses and strains of life.

4 Every man is constantly driven or inclined toward the fulfillment of his inborn needs and acquired wants. On the other hand, it is the common lot of all men to experience some measure of inadequacy, insecurity, anxiety, anger, or hostility in their efforts to achieve this fulfillment. When this occurs, your nature rallies spontaneously, i.e., without forethought or choice, to the support and defense of your disturbed sense of well-being. Consciously or unconsciously, you try to re-

move or change the conditions causing your inner disturbance. You usually do this through your personality structure, i.e., the individual habits and the habit-systems which make you the kind of person you are today. When a single habit is insufficient to solve some problem or conflict, you resort automatically to a habit system, i.e., a combination of habits working together toward a common goal.

5   No matter how you may feel about yourself, you cannot assume full credit or full blame for the sensitivities and habits that now direct most of your daily behavior. During your formative years, your inborn needs, acquired wants, and personal experiences played a large part in your personality formation. When touched or threatened by the unpleasant, your nature rallied spontaneously to sustain, protect, or restore your sense of well-being. Sometimes your nature did this by consciously suppressing facts, feelings, emotions, or memories, and turning her attention toward more satisfying objects or interests. When your experience was too upsetting to consider, your nature repressed the disturbing elements with the speed of lightning, and thereby prevented these elements from coming to your direct awareness. You

may have felt some vague uneasiness at that moment, but you could not understand why, because the upsetting matter was sidetracked before it could cause greater disturbance to your sense of well-being.

6 Thus, through the years, you developed your present habits of self-assertion, self-satisfaction, and self-protection. In its early stages, this development was largely conscious, but it was also partly unconscious through the process of repression just described above. In fact, even the conscious portion of this development gradually became unconscious to a large extent. This transformation took place through the formation of your habits. Even when you are aware that you are behaving under the influence of habit, you do not usually recall the original experiences which brought this habit into being. Neither do you understand how these habits have continued to influence your present behavior long after their original situations passed away. For example, some people approach life with a chip on their shoulder. This is their general attitude in many situations, even when it is unwarranted. The origin of this attitude can be traced to the conditions and circumstances of their

formative years. The young tree was bent this way often enough for the trunk to grow rigid in its curvature. So too with you. Your habitual behavior has become so much a part of you that you are hardly aware of it. Even when you do advert to it, you are usually too involved in maintaining or protecting your sense of well-being, to look at your behavior objectively, or to control it at the moment.

7 In view of these facts, is it any wonder that you should encounter some difficulties in striving for a fuller self-possession and a more objective self-management? In time of stress, your spontaneous nature is intent primarily on protecting itself from whatever threatens to hurt, upset, or oppress it. You are more strongly inclined to alleviate the stress caused by your feelings of inadequacy, insecurity, anxiety, or physical discomfort than about thinking the matter through and dealing with it intelligently. To complicate matters even more, your sense of well-being may also become concerned about moral principles and religious standards in your solution of stress. If so, you may find yourself caught between conflicting goals, namely, the satisfaction of your natural appetites or acquired wants, and the need to retain a

sense of well-being with your conscience. Your inner stress may become intensified by this situation. You may even feel momentarily like two different people in one, with your feelings going one way while your reason tends toward another direction.

8 This conflict between nature's spontaneous habits of self-satisfaction and her sincere desires to embrace truth and goodness, is not so strange or abnormal as it might seem. It is actually the experience of every man in a variety of situations. St. Paul describes it well in his letter to his Roman converts: "I cannot understand my own behavior. I fail to carry out the things I want to do, and I find myself doing the very things I hate. When I act against my own will, that means I have a self that acknowledges that the law is good, and so the thing behaving in that way is not myself but sin living in me. The fact is, I know of nothing good living in me—living, that is, in my unspiritual self—for though the will to do what is good is in me, the performance is not, with the result that instead of doing the good things I want to do, I carry out the sinful things I do not want." (Rom. 7:15-19)

9 On the other hand, St. Paul is clearminded enough to see that his spontaneous

tendencies and unwanted inclinations are not to be considered his fault. He calls them "sinful" because they are blind and disorderly, not because they bring condemnation down on him. He shows this in the following words: "When I act against my will, then, it is not my true self doing it, but sin which lives in me. In fact, this seems to be the rule, that every single time I want to do good, it is something evil that comes to hand. In my inmost self, I dearly love God's Law, but I can see that my body follows a different law that battles against the law which my reason dictates. This is what makes me a prisoner of that law of sin which lives inside my body." (Rom. 7:20-23)

10 In his confusion, Paul seems to doubt or blame himself, but not for long. He takes his doubts and sense of guilt, and places them in the hands of God by hoping and trusting in the merits of his divine Lord and Savior. He then sees himself more clearly and understands himself more fully. At this point, he acknowledges that both tendencies are part of him, but he also asserts that as long as he continues trying to live an orderly life, he need never worry about his blind disorderly inclinations. "What a wretched man I am!

Who will rescue me from this body doomed to death? Thanks be to God through Jesus Christ our Lord! In short, it is I who with my reason serve the Law of God, and no less I who serve in my unspiritual self the law of sin." (Rom. 7:24-25)

11 In proportion as you become convinced that this inner division of your nature is normal, rather than malicious, you will achieve a firmer peace of mind and spirit. Whether you feel disorderly emotions or unreasonable desires, or even fall involuntarily through ignorance, inadvertence, or weakness, you must be as fair-minded toward your self as you would want to be toward others. In your natural sensitivity to inner stress, your troubled sense of well-being may cause you some mental confusion or a momentary lack of self-control. If you center your attention only on this part of the process, you can waste both time and energy in needless anxiety and harmful self-doubts. Your wisest course would be to imitate St. Paul's example cited above. He made an honest decision about himself. He knew that his general desire was to fulfill the wisdom and goodness of God in his own behavior. Therefore he counterbalanced his confusing self-

doubts by stating his intention and maintaining a stubborn trust in Jesus.

12 Many of the obstacles mentioned above, stem from your nature's sensitivity to the stresses, strains, and frustrations of daily life. Your particular sensitivities stem from your bodily inheritance, early-life history, later emotional experiences, personality development, and the difficult or unpleasant situations of your present life. All of these factors have influenced your mind and spirit for years. Barring a miracle, you cannot change them in a short time, even with the best of intentions and noblest of efforts. Your first step toward an intelligent self-renewal lies in learning to tolerate the unavoidable stresses of life. You do this by seeing them as part of your everyday experiences, and by trying to follow your religious principles and moral judgments, in spite of contrary feelings, emotions, and inclinations. With this attitude and disposition, your daily efforts will gradually improve with God's help. You will even develop an intelligent willingness to fail in so far as God sees fit to permit this. As St. Paul saw so clearly, your intentions, efforts and faith make you a good person, while your failures do not necessarily make you a bad one.

22
Needs, Stress, and Solutions

1 IN TIME of stress, nature is spontaneously inclined to defend her sense of well-being. The greater the stress, the stronger the urge to restore nature's equilibrium. If the stress occurs often enough or severely enough, and a particular solution proves helpful, that solution will gradually become a habit. Even after the original stress situation is outgrown or forgotten, the solution may go on being applied to other situations through force of habit. This is also true of habit-systems. A habit-system is a team of habits joined together to achieve the solution of more complex problems and conflicts. Most of your successful solutions eventually become so automatic as to be utterly unconscious. That is, you no longer connect them with their original situations, but spontaneously apply them to all sorts of unpleasant situations.

2 When your habits of self-defense become this deeply rooted, they are difficult to change, and just about impossible to eliminate altogether. You have habits on every level of your being. You have bodily habits. For ex-

ample, you become hungry around your usual meal times. You have mental habits, which incline you to feel or think with rigid attitudes or prejudiced opinions. Your thought process is often swayed by your emotional views. These habits may even influence your moral principles and general outlook on life. In short, your habits play a strong part in the formation and inclinations of your personality. They make you the kind of person you are in your daily behavior. They incline you to be outgoing, withdrawn, or belligerent.

3 You may wonder how good or bad your habits are. That depends on how much they are in harmony with your total human nature. Each day you live on three levels at one and the same time. So intermingled are these levels that you are often unable to distinguish one from the other. When you have a toothache, you may tend to be grouchy with others. On the other hand, when you are upset over something, your body feels some tension and your thinking may not be so clear or balanced as usual. When you are busy studying or making plans for some project, your body eventually becomes tired. Your emotions may then tend to be more negative than usual. In proportion as your physical feelings, dis-

turbed emotions, or unrealistic imagination
control your thinking, the habits causing this
condition are bad. They prevent you from
following your better judgment.

4   This fact brings you face to face with the
first principle of true self-fulfillment. Your
nature is more than a mere bundle of uncon-
nected needs and wants. It is a complex unit
of interrelated parts, requiring an intelligent
order and balance in your efforts for self-
fulfillment. There is an objective primacy of
needs and wants in your nature. Among
your many needs, you have a primary need
to achieve satisfaction and contentment in
your daily performance. In proportion as this
satisfaction and contentment proceed from
an orderly perspective of life and an intelligent sense of values, your self-management
is realistic, healthy and morally good. For instance, your nature demands that you prefer
truth to falsehood. When truth is not too
clear or certain, your nature feels driven to
clarify the issue. Until this is done, your mind
will trouble you with its doubts, insecurity
and anxiety.

5   On the other hand, truth is not always attainable in its fullness. Sometimes this is due
to circumstances beyond your control. Some-

times, however, it is due to your emotional and mental habits. Every man has some habits which militate against his intelligent efforts for a fuller knowledge and understanding of life. These habits condition you in such a way as to make you minimize some things below their real importance, and magnify other things beyond their true value. This defective formation in your personality makes it difficult for you to achieve the order you would like to observe in your daily behavior. At such times, your feelings and emotions make it difficult for you to think clearly, judge wisely or act intelligently. Though you may know better, you are inclined to act worse in order to relieve yourself of the uneasiness, stress or frustration of the moment.

6 The better you understand yourself, so much the more will you be inclined to seek realistic solutions to your needs, wants and frustrations. Your only intelligent choice is, to make the most of your personal powers, such as they are with their physical limitations, mental blocks, and emotional obstacles. In proportion to your good will, you will seek help where possible. Your foremost desire ought to be to seek your present fulfillment with due respect for your nature as an adult

human being. Though your emotional habits can misdirect your thinking, try to see things in their true perspective, i.e., according to their proper place and importance. Your main conflict will be within yourself rather than with others. It will be between your old established undesirable habits and your new, desirable, but still weak motivations. Though God's grace is always at your disposal, you will still need time, practice, and experience to establish your new habits. Failure will be part of this experience. It will teach you how to overcome obstacles that hinder your present efforts.

7 Many, if not most, of your problems and conflicts stem from your unconscious needs and wants. We call them unconscious because, in varying degrees, they are hidden from your awareness. They were made unconscious through the process of repression, described in the preceding chapter. For some reason, they were so painful or disturbing to you that your self-defensive instinct prevented them from coming to your direct notice. In repression your mind may have registered some degree of uneasiness or tension, but the root source of the disturbance was not revealed openly to you. The repressed

material continues to make itself felt whenever it is in danger of being uncovered. It creates feelings, emotions, or other behavior out of proportion to the actual external situation occurring at the moment. For instance, you may find yourself disapproving of others, in order to counteract your own feelings of inferiority or guilt at their successful achievement. You may not be conscious of your inferiority or guilt feelings, but only of your disapproval. At the same time, you may not be able to explain why you feel so strongly about the matter in question.

8   The visible symptoms appearing in your behavior, are not usually your real problem. They are only the outward signs of an inner difficulty or frustration. The symptoms are nature's attempt to protect herself from the real, but hidden problem. Instead of trying to justify or deny the outward behavior, you ought to wonder why it occurs. You ought to ask yourself, what need are you trying to protect, what painful experience are you trying to escape? What inner problem makes you the victim of carelessness or over-cautiousness, inattention, or strained attention, slovenliness or perfectionism, boastfulness or inability to accept praise graciously,

rudeness or extreme politeness, hostility or shyness, aggressiveness or submissiveness? In any form of self-study, beware of morbid introspection, i.e., constantly looking for the worst in yourself. Strive to develop a scientific attitude, and your self-study will be more positive, more objective and relatively free of insecurity or anxiety.

9   The chief clues leading to a scientific self-understanding and self-acceptance, are your basic needs and wants. Physical needs are quite explicit in their demands. It is your mental, emotional, and spiritual needs and wants, that interfere most with your sense of well-being. By your very nature, you need to give some kind of free expression to your thoughts, feelings, and emotions. You have a constant need to exercise self-reliance, enjoy self-esteem, and earn the acceptance and approval of others. In varying degrees, every man needs to love and be loved, i.e., to give of himself to others, and to receive some measure of their good will, sympathetic communication and sincere appreciation of his self-giving. The preceding needs and wants might be summarized thus: Every man needs his personal measure of security, achievement, recognition and affection. These basic

needs are at the bottom of every disturbance
in man's sense of well-being.

10   You can strive for these natural and
normal goals with a realistic attitude or with
an unrealistic one. You can do your intelligent
and reasonable best to make the most of your
daily opportunities, and to respect the limitations that face you in each endeavor or
experience. On the other hand, you can refuse
to accept the unavoidable boundaries of your
efforts, and strain beyond your present
powers. You may try to strike back at others
with infantile hostility and aggressiveness. If
you do this, you must expect others to defend
themselves against you, each in his own way.
Even nature will have her revenge by upsetting your physical and mental health. Nature
demands order and balance. You contradict
her at your own expense. Since God is the
Author of Nature, you set yourself at odds
with Him when you disregard Nature's laws.

11   The wise man strives for a richer daily
life. He does it by seeking to maintain or
improve his self-possession and to achieve a
realistic self-management. This goal does not
take him out of his way. It only helps him
handle his daily problems and conflicts with
an adult view and a realistic attitude, as far

as his physical, emotional, and spiritual strength will permit, with the help of God's grace. To strive for more than this, is as childish and foolish as to strive for less.

23

The Problem of Adjustment

1 IN SPITE of your sincerest efforts to achieve an intelligent fulfillment of your needs and a reasonable satisfaction of your wants, be prepared to feel some insecurity, anxiety, frustration, or tension from time to time. Every man has his share of these. This does not mean that you cannot try to diminish them, but you must do so realistically, i.e., in accordance with the realities and principles which govern your human nature and your earthly life. The realistic man knows that life on earth is a mixture of pleasant and unpleasant, easy and difficult, fulfillment and frustration. He is intelligently disposed to accept the necessary bitter with the desirable sweet.

2 Deep within you, there is a constant drive to make your daily performance a satisfying experience. In your more reasonable mo-

ments, you would like to achieve your satisfaction through an intelligent adjustment to life's daily situations, problems, and opportunities. This realistic desire, however, is often frustrated to some degree, by your established negative habits. Though you know logically what to do, or how to act, you find yourself, often enough, doing or acting quite the contrary. Consequently, you cannot avoid some feelings of disappointment, discouragement, guilt, or anger, as you go about your daily routine. Unfortunately, you are not always conscious of these feelings and emotions. They are often submerged beneath the surface of your clear awareness. You may feel some vague uneasiness, dissatisfaction, or tension, without understanding why. You may even attribute these feelings or conditions to some particular person, place, thing, or situation which really has no connection with them.

3 Do not make the mistake of over-simplifying your view of life or of human nature. Your daily behavior is not always a matter of clear black and white, obvious good or bad, or evident right and wrong. Even when you know the answers, you cannot always be sure how they apply in some specific situations.

Though you may sincerely want to follow your conscience, you will sometimes have reason to doubt whether your conscience is presently based on sound intelligent principles or on unreasoning emotional motivations. The more you understand how your human nature is constructed and how it functions, so much the more will you also understand why some measure of mental confusion, emotional conflict, and moral weakness is normal to every man from time to time.

4 As you try to adjust intelligently to your daily problems, conflicts, and frustrations, you bring to these situations, not only your good will, enlightened by God's grace, but also your entire personal nature, with all its needs, wants, habits, and limitations. You are a marvelously complex being. Your bodily life is so intertwined with your mental, emotional, and rational functioning, that each of these levels of life affects each of the others, and is, in turn, affected by each of them. How you deal with each situation, depends not only on your measure of intelligence and will power, but also on your bodily health, mental development, emotional habits, moral training, and divine grace. Sometimes your physical energies make the difference between

your feeling secure in life's daily routine, and your feeling inadequate and anxious about the most ordinary performance. At other times, your emotional thinking may be too strong for your intellectual convictions, so that you may fear or reject facts and truth even while you desire to face them and live by them.

5 Barring extraordinary assistance from God, your adjustment to life's difficulties and inconveniences today, depends a good deal on the structure and dynamism of your personality. In other words, how you behave internally, perform externally, and react to life's daily situations, depends on your physical, mental, emotional, and spiritual constitution, with all your personal traits, needs, wants, attitudes, beliefs, values, motives, habits, and modes of adjusting to the varying circumstances of each day. This does not mean that you cannot change for the better in some area of life where change is definitely desirable or necessary. It means that you cannot assume possession of your own thinking and management of your own behavior without facing a period of effort and recurring failures against your established undesirable habits: You cannot begin a new chapter in

your life story, without feeling the effects of the previous chapters.

6 The more objective you can become in your self-study, the more you will be disposed to reconstruct the undesirable elements in your personality. Many people avoid any form of self-awareness for fear that it may upset their sense of well-being by arousing shame, disgust, guilt, or a fear of punishment. If they were more scientifically-minded, they would realize that their present personality-structure occurred long before they were in a position to help themselves. They were once so inadequate and dependent, that they had good reason to feel some degree of insecurity and anxiety on many occasions. What was an ant-hill to the adults on whom they depended, was often a mountain to the child. From the very nature of the situation, it was inevitable that some misunderstandings and misinterpretations should occur between adults and child. On these occasions, the child's sense of well-being was disturbed more frequently, and often more deeply, than most adults realized.

7 From earliest childhood, man is interested in the world around him. He is intensely curious about the nature and meaning of

what he sees, hears, and feels. He is moved by a restless desire for interesting and satisfying experiences. He is often in need of correction and assistance. During these early years, the child is constantly exposed to the emotional atmosphere of parents, siblings, and others. He soon learns to protect his sense of well-being, sometimes by complying with the expectations of others, sometimes by withdrawing from them, and sometimes by expressing some form of hostility. All of these efforts are attempts to adjust to each succeeding situation. Through trial and error, the growing child retains his satisfactory forms of adjustment, and rejects or modifies his other attempts. Through the years, these efforts become good adjustments or maladjustments, depending on whether or not they seek a realistic solution to the problems, conflicts, and frustrations.

8 Thus, your present daily efforts at self-possession and self-management are constantly directed toward maintaining or protecting your sense of well-being. At the same time, these efforts are strongly influenced by your non-rational feelings. In spite of your power to think logically and behave in accordance with your intelligence, you often

have to contend with your established emotional habits. These habits arise spontaneously whenever your sense of well-being is disturbed. In so far as they incline you to follow your reasonable nature, these habits are healthy and desirable. When, however, they incline you to disregard facts, truth, and basic moral principles, they endanger your true welfare. Moreover, these habits are often not only compelling, but also unconscious. They developed over a long period of time, and are so much a part of you that you cannot always achieve an easy focus on them and an unbiased evaluation of them. Finally, what makes these habits hard to reject or correct is the fact that they always bring you some momentary satisfaction or contentment.

9   Much as you may wish to be realistic in your everyday life, you must make due allowance for your established negative habits. They will not change quickly with a sincere resolution. Neither will they diminish easily through a determined, sustained effort. Undesirable though they be, these negative habits fulfill a real, but unrealistic need, because the sense of well-being they protect is not always in line with objective reality. Moreover, these habits often operate in a habit system. Conse-

quently, the habit you try to eradicate may be strengthened or required by some other habit of which you are not even aware. Thus, as you strive to conquer a particular bad habit, you may find yourself forgetting to work at it, seeking reasons to defend it, or simply finding excuses to delay its conquest.

10   The first intelligent step out of this unhealthy situation, is to realize what it means to be human. Man is imperfect by his very nature. He has many natural limitations and shortcomings. In themselves, none of these may be a cause for shame or blame. They are simply a part of you. You must accept yourself and respect yourself for what you are. Secondly, you need not fear self-knowledge. What you are, you are, and thinking differently about yourself won't change what you really are. It takes work, patience, and time to change some of your personal defects. Others may not be changeable at all. Thirdly, learn to appreciate whatever good qualities you possess and whatever good you may yet accomplish, be these ever so limited. A reasonable contentment with self will incline you to look on others more kindly. As you radiate good will toward others, they may sense something of God's nearness through your

spirit. They may not be aware of this directly. They may simply feel well-disposed toward their neighbor or toward life in general. In so doing, they spread the spirit of love and kindness, which you communicated to them by your good will and God's grace.

11   The basic virtue which you need for a healthy adjustment to life is the virtue of humility. It disposes you to be realistic, i.e., to see things as they are and live life as reasonably as you are able in your present circumstances. Under the influence of humility, you will prefer to invest the one or two talents which God has entrusted to you, rather than bury your meager gifts in the ground of negative feelings and emotions, e.g., inadequacy-feelings, insecurity, anxiety, self-pity, fear of failure, or hostility toward yourself or others. When Jesus ordered His disciples to collect the crumbs and crusts left over after his multiplication of food for the hungry crowd, He taught how even left-overs can be used for further purposes. Think like Him, and you will never underestimate the achievement that you may yet perform in this life.

12   It is far better to improve a small, but real situation, than to perform great deeds in

mere wishful imagination. Though you may yearn for higher achievements, do not neglect the lesser achievements within your grasp. When you feel too "little" or "unimportant," consider how the whole universe is composed of tiny atoms, each making its own specific contribution to the existence and functioning of the whole wide universe. Would you do less? Then, indeed, would you have cause for shame. On a dark night, even a little spark gives some light. Do not let your light remain unused. Light it and direct it to the path or task before you. You can then find some joy in the fact that you lived with whatever you had, and did what little was possible to you. God is reasonable. He asks only that you adjust to reality, i.e., fit your personality, such as it is, to your present circumstances, such as they are. Then make the most of your situation and opportunities. Through such realistic self-adjustment, you will achieve your fullest possible growth and your broadest possible fulfillment both here and hereafter.

24
Flight From Reality

IF YOU study the habits of living things, you will quickly notice how the vast majority of them spontaneously turn away from any danger or threat to their well-being. Human nature behaves the same way. When faced with any form of disturbance or threat, man's first urge is to avoid or run from the situation. Escape is usually the quickest, easiest, and safest form of self-defense. Sometimes it is also the wisest way to preserve one's well-being. Often enough, however, flight merely creates fresh problems or new conflicts. When this happens, the wise man strives to achieve an acceptable solution to his frustration or conflict. The greater your insight into the objective situation, the more apt you will be to work toward a realistic solution. In the following paragraphs you will find various solutions which often bring more harm than help. Every human being employs one or more of them from time to time. When, however, they become habitual and are applied unconsciously and automatically to unpleasant situations, they limit one's power to think clearly and control his ability to manage his behavior intelligently.

2   Some people prefer to live in the past, rather than adjust to unavoidable changes in the present. Their sense of well-being is disturbed by new situations, and their sense of security is upset by changing attitudes and customs. Feeling unable to cope with their inner disturbance, they seek consolation or self-assurance in daydreams about their "better days" or bygone achievements. With faded memories, or unconscious repression of the unpleasant, they convince themselves that the present lacks many or most of the good qualities of the past.

3   The truth of the matter is that every generation has its own vices and its own virtues. With each passing generation, human history adds a few more pages to man's earthly experience, a few more chapters to his book of knowledge, and a few more horizons to his view of earthly living. The evolution of the world is never at a standstill. The old is not better for being old, nor is the new better for being new. The wise man selects the best from both old and new, puts them together, and enriches his life by a balanced use of both.

4   There are people who never grow beyond

a certain stage in their personality development. They seem unable to break out of their emotional attitudes of childhood, or to progress beyond their adolescent responses to life's daily problems and conflicts. In a crisis, they fail to apply their advanced school learning or to learn from their personal experience. Like children, they respond with excessive compliance, fear, anger, or hate. They may even give a good rational argument in favor of their behavior, but they are neither peacefully convinced by their own reasoning nor easily helped by external correction or direction. They may even disapprove of others who have this same problem, without being aware that they have it themselves. Their unconscious repression makes it well-nigh impossible for them to help themselves. Whatever their good will, it needs to be directed by a wise counsellor, toward a healthy growth of mind and spirit.

5   Some people crowd out their awareness of unacceptable facts and situations by dreaming about possible future achievements. In fantasy they see themselves performing glorious deeds and winning the admiration and praise of others. In real life they are blind to the most obvious duties and chores that

lie around them undone. They put off these tasks until the very last possible moment. Only under pressure can these people perform their duties and fulfill their obligations. If they started sooner, their performance would be charged with mental uneasiness and physical tension. The time would seem so long, and the work would appear so difficult. as to become well nigh intolerable. Having experienced this strain before, these people look forward to future performances with dread of its repetition.

To some people, the above explanation may seem like nonsense or a weak excuse. And yet, everyone has had some experience of this in varying degrees. Everyone has his preferences and prejudices in any choice of achievements. Each man will automatically lean toward the activity which most appeals to him. In proportion as an occupation or activity promises fulfillment to your sense of well-being, you will find yourself liking it more than other alternatives. In proportion as it arouses feelings of inadequacy, inse- curity, anxiety, or frustration, it will disturb your sense of well-being and arouse your dislike. If this negative experience is felt in- tensely enough or often enough, you will look forward to each repetition with a dread of the strain involved. Your very expectation will add to the unpleasantness of future recurrences of the experience.

7   Some people resort to fantasy and daydreams either as a substitute for actual accomplishment or as a consolation for their poor or non-existent performance. They imagine themselves as able, but unwilling to perform. In these dreams, they imagine themselves possessing a power, virtue, or talent that raises them above the common throng. In their need to preserve their sense of well-being, they unconsciously choose to enjoy the limitless perfection of imagined superiority, rather than face a possible disappointment in a real, but limited achievement. If the unpleasant truth forces itself on them, some people will admit their failures, but will protect their sense of well-being by blaming other people or unfavorable circumstances. Thus even in failure, these people will see themselves as innocent victims falling heroically in a noble effort for higher goals.

8   Some people try to distract themselves from unpleasant self-awareness by escaping into a whirlwind of external activity. They forget their personal problems by fixing their

attention on the problems and needs of others. They feel useful, needed, and praiseworthy, as they give time and energy to alleviating the troubles and sufferings of their fellow-man. Others may take refuge from inner stress, by an intense pre-occupation with some hobby or sport. Finally, there are people who seek relief from life's daily pressures through an excessive use of alcohol, tobacco, food, drugs, or some other form of bodily indulgence. In moderation, one or other of these means might be of some assistance, but in excess they can do more harm than good. Unfortunately, when one's inner stress or pain is great, he may easily tend to counter-balance it with excessive doses.

9   Finally, when faced with any truth or reality which might arouse your sense of inadequacy, insecurity, or anxiety, your nature may resort to another means of escaping inner stress. It may employ the process of mental dissociation. By this process, your mind is unconsciously compelled to view your behavior, not as a whole, but in segregated fragments. It sees each fragment as a separate unit, cut off from your contrary behavior in other circumstances. In this way, your mind is prevented from facing any in-

consistency or contradiction in your total
behavior. In short, this mental process pro-
tects your sense of well-being from any upsetting self-doubts or guilt feelings.

10   In varying degrees, everyone uses dissociation as a form of self-defense at one time
or another. It performs a real, though unhealthy, function in your nature's constant
drive, to maintain her sense of well-being.
This process makes it possible for a man to
be sincerely eager to praise and please God
on Sunday, and just as sincerely ready to
violate the principles of justice and charity in
his week-day business practices. He is moved
to do both as a protection of his sense of well-
being. It would upset him to feel separated
from God, and it would upset him to feel
threatened or hurt by others in business.
Moreover, it would also upset him to see the
humiliating inconsistency between these two
contrary motives. Therefore, his nature re-
presses this fact of inconsistency, before his
mind can see it clearly. In a word, he needs
to feel equally safe and satisfied in his dealings with God, his business, and his own
self-management. Unconscious repression enables him to dissociate each item of his behavior from any other conflicting item within

himself. If he did this consciously, he would be guilty of hypocrisy or presumption on God's mercy.

11   This subject of mental dissociation may sometimes make one feel some uneasiness or discomfort. This is to be expected. Every man has his moments of self-doubts, insecurity, or anxiety about his true welfare both here and hereafter. Many people are afraid that they may be deceiving themselves knowingly and freely. They cannot look at facts without making them exclusively a matter of sin or virtue. And yet, this subject of man's flight from reality must be viewed as completely as possible, if you are to achieve a fuller self-understanding and assume a greater self-management in the future.

12   There may be times when flight from some situation is wise or necessary. When this is so, do not be ashamed to leave. No man is obliged to the impossible. True, you may see such a situation as an opportunity to suffer or die for a worthy cause. Your decision may be formed on an overly emotional judgment or on a special grace from God. By and large, however, you would be wise to refrain from acting when your emotions are strong, and the issue is too deep or too broad for an

adequate judgment. Take your problem to God in prayer, and do not hesitate to consult others with more knowledge, experience, wisdom, and prudence than the average person. Seek to know the truth, not merely as you see it, but as nearly as possible, as it really is.

13   It may take you some time before you become habitually aware that the mechanisms mentioned above are not so rare as most people think. In varying degrees, they are part of everybody's daily experience. They occur both within you and within those with whom you deal. Sometimes they are so mild as to go unnoticed, sometimes they stand out unmistakably. While it is not advisable to be overly analytical of each and every item in your behavior or that of others, it is just as undesirable to be insensitive and unappreciative of the deeper needs and wants influencing your interpersonal communications. Your understanding will make you reasonably sympathetic and intelligently well-disposed both toward yourself and those with whom you deal. With this fuller view of human nature, you will be more like God, Who measures each man's external behavior by the internal forces from whence it proceeds

Though you will never plumb the depths of human nature, you can become more tolerant of its weaknesses.

14 Your daily life is your personal contribution to the evolution of God's creation in this world. Live it with knowledge, wisdom, prudence, and a healthy respect for the limitations you meet within yourself and within others. God wants you to be yourself, but not a narrow-minded, inconsiderate self, with no feeling for the necessary needs and legitimate wants of those around you. As creation requires the constant support of the divine presence, so does your routine world need whatever support you can provide by your spirit of understanding, compassion, and reasonable concern for others. Be you ever so faint a reflection of the Divine Goodness, you will have made your world a little brighter for your having come this way.

25

Unhealthy Defense Mechanisms

1 TRY AS you may, you cannot solve every problem nor settle every conflict. Though you know this intellectually, your nature will still incline you to defend yourself against

every person, thing, or situation that upsets your sense of well-being. Your nature's first urge may be to escape, but she is just as quick to resist, or even attack, if she feels intolerably threatened, frustrated, or hurt. Like your flight mechanisms, your defense mechanisms are so habitual that they operate spontaneously and unconsciously. Whatever your conscious intentions, your deepest and most basic motive in any behavior or endeavor is always the fulfillment of your needs and wants, and the preservation of your sense of well-being. Even when you are moved to help others, what you feel immediately is your concern for them and your need or desire to help. You are not always explicitly aware of this ever-present motivation. Nevertheless, it is the main root of every voluntary choice and involuntary behavior of yours.

2   You may feel reluctant to admit that your best intentions and highest motives always involve some degree of self-interest. You may sincerely desire to strip yourself of all self-seeking, and to direct your energies selflessly toward some worthy cause. Whatever your conscious preferences, you cannot detach them entirely from your basic self-concern. In fact, you cannot even become concerned

about any person, object, or purpose, unless you have somehow identified them with yourself, or yourself with them. Thus, your deepest feelings, emotions, and external behavior not only originate from your predominant needs and wants, but they also bring some fulfillment to these same needs and wants in every achievement. In other words, in every act of spontaneous and voluntary self-giving, you achieve some measure of self-satisfaction and fulfillment. True, your motives may be unrealistic and your intentions misguided, but until you are aware of this, you will remain content.

3   The fact that your nature is congenitally self-centered, is no cause for shame. This is both natural and normal. It's how you direct your self-concern, that makes you infantile or adult, foolish or wise, bad or good. Man's primary tendency is to seek his fulfillment in reality and truth, rather than in pretense and falsehood. In other words, man normally prefers "the real thing" in his search for satisfaction and contentment. It is only when reality and truth seem impossible to achieve or intolerably difficult to face, that man will turn to unrealistic substitutes. In proportion as his sense of well-being is disturbed or frustrated,

his mind is seized by a sense of insecurity and anxiety; his body responds with physical tension and physiological malfunctioning; and his spirit finds difficulty in thinking clearly and behaving intelligently. Under the influence of his frustrated needs and wants, man reaches out for whatever may relieve his internal pressures or protect him from external harm. At such times, his predominant concern is the defense or restoration of his sense of well-being. Unless a stronger goal can move him in a different direction, he feels some measure of compulsion to resort to one or more of the following self-defenses.

4   Some people find it extremely difficult to accept whatever threatens or disturbs their self-esteem. In their need to see themselves in harmony with their self-ideal, and to avoid self-doubts or guilt-feelings, they unconsciously center their attention on their good qualities, and remain blind to their defects and faults. Any suggestion offered for their improvement, arouses their objections, resentments, or counterattacks. Some of those having this problem, are so afraid of being hurt by the criticism or observations of others, as to shun any close involvements with most or all of the people around them. They keep

their distance by maintaining a neutral attitude toward others and toward life in general.

5 Some people protect themselves from their own insecurity and anxiety through a "reaction-formation." They unconsciously adopt feelings and behavior which express the direct opposite of their original tendencies. Thus, an apparent extrovert may really be a deep introvert who is trying to forget his intolerable self-awareness through external distractions and interests. The overly agressive person may be a very timid man trying to counteract his unbearable feelings of insecurity and anxiety. The compliant person may really be trying to keep control of his deeper spontaneous tendency to dominate or outshine others. By behaving compliantly, he feels protected from the possible hostility and rejection which he might arouse by following his original inclination to get the upper hand.

6 Some people are so afraid of performing unsatisfactorily, that they adopt the physical symptoms of some illness or injury. These symptoms help them save face either with themselves or with others, when they feel unable to fulfill their routine obligations or achieve some particular goal. This self-defense is adopted so unconsciously, that

these people really feel the discomfort of their symptoms. Their aches and pains really hurt, due to the physical tensions aroused by their keen sense of insecurity and anxiety. Some will even avoid pleasant activities, e.g., dancing, swimming, or other sports. They are so self-conscious that they feel sure that everyone else is observing or commenting on their poor performance. All of these people limit themselves to a very controlled routine and to a small number of persons with whom they feel accepted.

7 Another defense mechanism is that of "dissimulation." Some people spontaneously act out the opposite of what they really feel deep down within themselves. Openly, they may show disgust or sorrow over stories involving dishonesty, violence, sex, etc. At the same time, they may sense within themselves some vague attraction toward such subjects. For instance, a prudish person may actually have a deep curiosity about sexual matters, or may be strongly attracted by the physical qualities of others. These deeper inclinations may be so well hidden in the depths of his mind, that he may be quite unaware of his real feelings. The repression of his real feelings occurs so spontaneously and compul-

sively as to prevent self-directed feelings of insecurity, anxiety, doubt, or guilt, or avoid possible rejection, humiliation, or punishment from others.

8 Some people have a strong need to explain any behavior of theirs that may seem questionable. They are always ready to give a "good reason" for their attitudes or conduct. Sometimes this self-defense goes on entirely within their own minds. They explore every possible reason, argument, or excuse in an effort to keep their self-image in line with their self-ideal. They simply must see themselves matching their ideal. Only then can they maintain their self-esteem and preserve their sense of well-being. This "rationalizing" gives them the "good reasons" they need for having followed, or for continuing to follow, feelings, emotions, desires, or any other behavior which may seem or be questionable. Their primary concern is not always to convince others. It is more often a matter of saving face within themselves. By reconciling their self-image with their self-ideal, they avoid or diminish their disturbing sense of self-doubt or guilt.

9 Rationalizing is applied in a variety of situations. Thus, some people profess to be

"glad" or "lucky", when they fail to achieve some desired goal. They try to convince themselves or others, that the goal really was not worthwhile after all. It might upset them too much to admit that they missed a good thing. The truth would arouse their feelings of self-disgust, guilt, or fear of what others might say or think about their effort. Other people may rationalize in the opposite direction. They may claim that their failure was actually "not so bad." Though they did not intend these results, they will insist that the matter turned out for the better.

10   Then again there are those who try to counterbalance their inadequacy and inferiority feelings by finding fault with other individuals, races, groups, institutions, or achievements. In the real or imagined shortcomings and failures of others, these people find company for their own misery, or see grounds for feeling less disturbed about their own shortcomings. There are some people who simply cannot accept responsibility for their own defects or failures. They excuse themselves by blaming others, or by blaming their own unfortunate circumstances. Their sense of well-being is so insecure, that any admission of limitations or defects would be

intolerable to them. They would immediately be besieged by numerous doubts, guilt, fear of punishment, etc. Their mind would not rest until it was utterly exhausted by endless self-scrutiny and self-questioning.

11   Some people refuse to face life as is. They insist on seeing it as an injustice to them. Instead of taking a realistic view of their present situation, and studying how they may yet make something of themselves in their present circumstances, they unconsciously convince themselves that they never had a chance. They base their negative attitude on this conviction, and refuse to help themselves. They constantly do poorly in their undertakings, sometimes through a thorough lack of self-confidence and sometimes through an unconscious need to justify their negative attitude by further failure. They have a fear that any success might oblige them to continue striving. Such an obligation would arouse their feelings of inadequacy, insecurity, and anxiety. The strain of a sustained effort would be too much for them. So, unconsciously they prefer to excuse themselves from life's daily struggle as best they can.

12   Finally, there are people who alleviate their emotional disturbances and physical

tensions by "taking it out" on the people, things, and situations around them. By attacking these scapegoats, they diminish their own sense of inadequacy, inferiority, insecurity, anxiety, hostility, or guilt. They have to explode at something or someone other than themselves. So, they aim their inner pressures at these external targets. Any attempt to have these people consider the real source of their inner upsets and tensions, tends to fail, because they unconsciously dread self-awareness. It arouses too much self-doubt, mental confusion, and emotional turmoil in them. They find some sort of self-unity in maintaining a state of war against their environment. Moreover, they also achieve some alleviation to their inner uneasiness and tensions.

13 It is important for you to realize that every man has his occasional urges to resort to some of these unhealthy self-defenses. These are the roots of human misunderstandings, interpersonal friction, and social injustices. There can be no lasting renewal within individuals or communities unless it begins with a deep appreciation of the inner dynamism of human nature itself. Even the man who turns to God, needs an intelligent

understanding of himself and his neighbor, if he is to make a balanced and reasonable use of the inspirations and graces bestowed on him from above. True, God can work miracles within the soul of any man, but this is not His ordinary way of dealing with human nature. This is seen in the Gospel accounts of the different Apostles. Each one retained his natural personal traits, even after being called to follow the Master. Only the miraculous transformation of Pentecost changed them beyond the limits of "ordinary, everyday grace."

14 You must not depend on a miracle for your self-renewal. You need to work from day to day for a realistic, grace-supported growth toward Christian Maturity. This growth will not take you the least bit away from your daily occupations and obligations. It is part of what you are, feel, think, and do. You yourself have a deep, maybe even unconscious, desire to be respected by yourself and others. Moreover, you want the respect to be truthful, i.e., rightly deserved. No man likes to think of himself as a "fraud." When Jesus prayed for His followers, He asked His heavenly Father to "Sanctify them in truth." Do not fear the truth. It will not demand more

of you than you are able to achieve. It will not take you unreasonably out of your way, but will guide you along your daily path and show you how it may be followed intelligently and reasonably. True, some of your established habits will block your efforts toward a more adult behavior, and you will see many a partial or total failure in your efforts. You need only to keep trying, and leave all else in the hands of God. If you are man enough to do this, you are man enough for God and for all others who know how to value a proven sincerity.

26

Adjustment Through Compensation

THE ART of earthly living is the art of adjusting to life's daily situations. In proportion as your predominant needs and wants are satisfied and your sense of well-being prevails, you enjoy emotional contentment, peace of mind, and spiritual vitality. When this condition prevails, you feel disposed to face life's daily activities, situations, and problems realistically. Unfortunately, your fulfillment and well-being depend on a number of people, things, and circumstances over which you have a limited control or no control at all. Consequently, some frustrations and conflicts are inevitable. This is man's natural condition in this world. The more able you are to view this condition as normal, so much the more will you be disposed to adjust to the changing situations of each passing hour. With this attitude, you will try to make the most of your real abilities and opportunities when the unexpected or unpleasant comes your way.

2 Nature has a way of compensating for her deficiencies. Plant life tends to adapt to the natural conditions in which it exists. Animals naturally adapt to the changing weather conditions and food problems of each succeeding season. In his own way, man also undergoes an evolution of body, mind, and spirit, as he proceeds through life. Even in civilized society, the struggle for fulfillment and survival goes on. Amid the variety of personal habits, local customs, racial ties, and international organizations, man is still bent on seeking his fulfillment and preservation through some kind of conscious adjustment to reality.

3 When flight from life's problems seems too difficult, and the mental mechanisms mentioned in the previous chapter, seem in-

adequate to solve prevailing conflicts, man
naturally resorts to some form of compensation. He seeks an acceptable substitute to
counteract whatever is threatening or disturbing his sense of well-being. An obvious
example is that of a boy who cannot equal his
brother's scholastic attainments. He may
strive to compensate by excelling in athletic
achievements. The admiration of others and
his inner satisfaction with his athletic performance counterbalance his disturbing feelings of inferiority or envy of his brother.
Compensation is a natural phenomenon. It
occurs so frequently in daily life, that people
usually fail to recognize it, whether in themselves or in others. In so far as it is realistic,
it can be a wise and constructive solution for
a number of problems. On the other hand,
compensation is often unconscious, compulsive, and unrealistic. In this case it is an
obstacle to one's own fulfillment, and a
hindrance to the well-being of others.

4   Man learns the use of compensation at an
early age. In childhood he is constantly aware
of his inadequacy to provide for his needs and
wants. Through his formative years, his dependency on others makes itself felt in a
million ways. It is only natural that he should

seek the assistance and re-assurance of his elders, whenever his sense of well-being is threatened or disturbed. In proportion to his inadequacy, and dependency, he sees his elders as pillars of knowledge, wisdom, and strength. Since he really needs them, he cannot help identifying them with his security and well-being. In his need of their acceptance and approval, he adopts their way of thinking and feeling about many things. With advancing age and experience, the growing child gradually spreads his identification to other grown-ups who make a favorable impression on him, e.g., other relatives, teachers, heroes, God. This identification plays a major role in the development of his attitudes, personal standards, and conscience.

5 Eventually the child reaches a new horizon. In his evolving drive toward greater independence and fuller self-expression, he feels a growing need to be acceptable to himself as well as to others. Identifying himself with others is no longer enough. In his yearning for an inner sense of individuality, he imagines himself as actually possessing the knowledge, wisdom, strength, and other admirable qualities of those whom he needs or admires the most. It is not a case of mere

imagination, but of a strong need to believe that he really possesses these desirable qualities. This mental operation is called introjection. It occurs outside of, and beyond one's conscious awareness. It is a natural outgrowth of identification and aims at the same final goal, i.e., a fuller and firmer sense of well-being. The developing person no longer looks on his desires and goals as a fulfillment of the expectations of others, but as his own personal need and choice. This sense of personal desire and choice enables him to develop and maintain his self-esteem. Many a personality likeness between adults and children, develops from this form of compensation.

6 Another form of compensation is called projection. It is a kind of reverse introjection. As the growing individual tries to develop the desirable qualities of his elders and heroes, he also tries to remedy or reject his own unacceptable traits. Before he even notices the presence of these unwanted qualities within himself, he tends to repress his disturbing awareness or feelings. This process is so automatic, compulsive, and swift, as to operate outside and beyond one's clear and explicit awareness. In proportion as his

process of repression weakens in any particular area of his insecurity or anxiety he strengthens it through the added process of introjection. He now proceeds to defend himself not only by fearing or hating these qualities within himself, but also within others. The more he fears these qualities in others, the more prone is he to suspect others, or even to accuse them of having these disturbing traits. He is like the pot calling the kettle black before he himself can be attacked for his own real or imagined blackness. This process helps him protect himself not only from the disapproval of others, but also from his own self-directed hostility.

7 Even when forced to acknowledge negative qualities in himself, one may need to ease his feelings of inferiority, guilt, or anxiety by finding fault with people around him or with the circumstances in which he lives. Such fault-finding helps him improve his own self-image by tearing down the image of others. Some people have this tendency especially toward their superiors or others who have, or seem to have superior qualities. Even when criticism is aimed at the real defects of others, they are made without due allowance for understandable human error or

for normal human limitations. Consciously or unconsciously, the critic is too busy trying to forestall his own inner feelings of inadequacy, insecurity, or anxiety, to divert any positive feelings toward his victim. This urge to find fault, is a form of compensation for his crumbling self-assurance or self-esteem.

8   Sometimes one's emotions may be utterly frustrated. Either the object of his desire is unattainable, or the clutches of his fear are inescapable, or finally, the target of his hostility is unassailable. In a word, to direct his emotion toward its real internal object, would create a greater anxiety than he now experiences. The more intolerable this situation becomes, the more urgently is his nature compelled to restore or defend her sense of well-being. Nature may attempt a solution by diverting the frustrated emotion from the impossible self-expression toward a more attainable one. This spontaneous maneuver of nature is achieved outside and beyond one's conscious awareness. The emotional feelings are displaced from the actual internal object, and transferred to a substitute and external one. The person involved in this maneuver, may know how strongly he feels about the external object, but he cannot

account for the intensity of his displaced emotion. The original source of these feelings is buried deep beneath his conscious mental view.

9   This compensation by displacement has the immediate advantage of alleviating the prevailing intensity of insecurity and anxiety. On the other hand, it also has the disadvantage of making self-possession and self-management more difficult than before. This unconscious displacement of emotions makes one less capable of seeing the people and things around him in their proper perspective. Whatever reasons he may give consciously for his prevailing attitudes and emotions toward life's daily experiences, his real reasons are hidden too deep for him to recognize or rectify. His efforts to love his neighbor, or to right the wrongs of others, are governed more by his unconscious reasons than by his conscious sincere application to the situation at hand. His unconscious emotions can unbalance his attitudes and distort his views in his daily endeavor to contribute to the world around him. Though he may be utterly blameless for his imbalance or distortion, others will suffer for it in some way. His avowed love of justice may actually be a

disguised unconscious need to express hostility and practice aggression against others.

10   Some people compensate for their feelings of inadequacy, insecurity, and anxiety by concentrating their attention on themselves. They are keenly sensitive about their health, looks or any notable quality which they see or imagine in themselves. Explicitly or implicitly, they magnify their own accomplishments or endeavors. Their conversation is one constant declaration or defense of how they feel about people and things. Conversely, they seem to lack interest or regard for the feelings, thinking, efforts, or achievements of others. Only in so far as they need others, do they allow themselves to become involved. Even in their religious efforts, they practice first and foremost a deep concern for their own fulfillment and well-being. Other people are simply the tools they need for self-fulfillment. They measure their self-giving by how much it proves their worth or brings them admiration, praise, and glory. You might be tempted to consider these people utterly "selfish" in a moral sense. Many of them, however, are narcissistic, i.e., unconsciously emotionally self-centered. They are so full of insecurity and anxiety that they are generally

unable to extend their concern and energies outwardly toward others. They are obsessively and compulsively preoccupied with maintaining or defending their sense of well-being. They simply have little or no energy to spare for others.

11   Some people try to compensate for their feelings of insecurity and anxiety by assuming a habitual attitude of hostility. Their sense of inadequacy and self-doubt generates mental uneasiness and physical tensions. This condition makes them ultra-sensitive to external pressures, real or imagined. What the average man sees as ordinary routine experience, the insecure man sees as a test of his ability or even as a challenge. With such a view of life, he cannot prevent himself from feeling constantly threatened. His nature is apprehensive much or most of the time. He is bound by a sense of self-doubt and insecurity with others. This condition gradually leads to anger and resentment. He may be disposed to direct his anger outwardly at others. If he is unable to do this, he may direct his anger inwardly against himself. The sadist finds some relief to his inner tensions by striking out at others. The masochist finds relief in punishing himself or being punished by others. These un-

healthy forms of compensation can be employed in numberless ways and countless degrees. The subject himself may be utterly unaware of the real cause of his hostile attitudes and behavior.

12   Some people express their hostility by mischievous behavior. They are prone to do things which are generally annoying to others, or explicitly forbidden. They seem to be utterly unconcerned about other people's feelings. And yet, consciously or unconsciously, the mischief-maker is very concerned. His mischief may be aimed at gaining attention, even if it be unfavorable attention. Whether he be criticized, blamed, or punished, he finds some sort of satisfaction in the attention he is getting. He no longer feels ignored. He now feels like a "somebody" with whom others must reckon. Some mischief-makers literally look for trouble to draw them out of their inner misery. They feel "all tied up," or "hemmed in" by their constant monotonous feelings of inadequacy, inferiority, insecurity, anxiety, or frustrated hostility. The opposition or resentment of others arouses the mischief-maker to defend his already desperate self. This defense is a relief to his intolerable inner boredom.

Other mischief-makers are simply "getting back" at others, whom they see as the cause of their problems or tensions. And finally, some mischief-makers see their mischief as a proof of superiority. The constant joker, teaser, or challenger fits into this general category of "mischief-maker," even if only on a superficial level. We might sum up the mischief-maker thus: In his mischievous behavior, he feels a satisfying sense of compensation, which he lacks when trapped within the intolerable routine of his negative emotions and attitudes.

13   Some people compensate for their feelings of insecurity and anxiety by relying on fetishes, e.g., good-luck charms, four-leaf clovers, or any other token to which they attach a superstitious value. Religious people sometimes act in this manner through an unreasoning, emotional attachment to religious articles, particular prayers, or certain good works. Though these religious symbols and actions have an objective value of their own, these people use them as "emotional proofs" of their faith, hope, sorrow for sin, or love of God. They lack the peaceful conviction and calm balance of one who relies on the gift of God's grace, and trusts in the

redeeming merits of the Divine Savior. They therefore need these visible external objects or actions to convince themselves of their own sincerity and acceptability to God.

14   One of the most widespread forms of compensation for one's deficiencies or faults, is the use of psychic symbols. For instance, a flag, a diploma, a uniform, or even a family name, can arouse certain attitudes, sentiments, or dispositions in a person. Every man associates certain persons, places, things or situations with his inner sense of inadequacy, insecurity, anxiety, hostility, identification. What makes these objects psychic symbols, is their "meaning" to each individual respectively. Symbols are employed by each and every human being. The very name or idea of God, goodness, virtue, sin, death, success, failure, etc., may arouse noble sentiments in one individual, negative feelings in another, and outright repugnance or hostility in someone else. The status symbol of one man, may be a source of shame or guilt feeling to his neighbor. Though symbols can be helpful when conscious, deliberate, and constructive, they can also create problems and conflicts when unconscious, compulsive, and negative.

15 Finally, it is impossible for anyone to have his needs, wants, and desires fulfilled every time they assert themselves. Sometimes you are expected or required to control yourself with due consideration for the legitimate needs and wants of others. At other times, you may feel obliged to listen to your own intelligence, as it objects to your blind following of spontaneous urges or unreasoning desires. In a variety of occasions, you meet some sort of frustration. Though the need or want is frustrated against your will, or controlled with your full consent, you still face the pent-up energy of the original drive, urge, or desire. If you allow your attention to dwell on that energy, you may stir up a stronger urge, and finally surrender to it. The wise thing to do is to relieve your tension by using the pent-up energy for less harmful or more acceptable purposes. This internal process of self-management is called "sublimation."

16 Sublimation sometimes occurs in you spontaneously, automatically, and even unconsciously. Sometimes, it is employed not only consciously, but also deliberately. In either case it is nature's endeavor to put your unreasoning inner forces to more useful, or less destructive use. In a sense, sublimation is the opposite of rationalization. Instead of trying to give yourself a good reason for doing a bad thing, you try to divert ill-advised energies toward more realistic goals. A child will refuse to frustrate his unhealthy tendencies, unless his sense of well-being becomes upset by these tendencies. He will be troubled only in proportion as he sees his urge primarily as a threat to his well-being. The mature man sees his misguided spontaneous urges, not only as threats to his sense of well-being, but also as potential obstacles to the legitimate welfare of others. In either case, however, the frustrated energies may require some kind of expression. If the original unacceptable tendency is too much a part of one's personality for him to disregard it, he may have to direct it toward a permanent and satisfying goal, e.g., by becoming a good salesman, an outstanding athlete, a dedicated teacher, etc. With such a realistic solution, one may serve both his undeniable need and the needs of his community. An immature person might see his solution in becoming a dishonest salesman, a dominating teacher, etc. In any case, he cannot quite manage his predominant emotions toward an orderly fulfillment.

17 The forms of compensation mentioned in this chapter, occur more frequently than many people realize. Every man has his habitual pattern of compensation. Even the man who makes a sincere effort to construct a wise pattern has his weak spots. Man is simply too human to achieve a complete self-understanding and a perfect self-management in this life. Your only intelligent hope lies in trying to live each day as reasonably and wisely as you can. Your true maturity is proven, not by a constant, perfect achievement, but in a realistic daily desire to become acquainted with your God-given limits through your shortcomings, mistakes, and failures. As you come to know your limits, you can either refuse to acknowledge them, or learn to live within them. If you choose the first alternative, you prove yourself a child, whatever your chronological age. If you work toward the second alternative, you will be proving yourself a true adult, i.e., one who wishes to live in accordance with the truth, facts, and realities that govern his daily life. Do not build your life on the false philosophy of "All or none." Only God is All, and every man is a limited participant in the divine All-ness.

18 If you listen to your "feelings" about your personal worth, merit, achievement, or eternal destiny, you may have a few doubts about where you stand in the divine plan of your life. Jesus said that one ought put his hand to the plough, and look ahead, not backwards, as he moves slowly toward the task at hand. (Luke 9:62) Whatever your age, experience, or learning here on earth, you will never see the day when you can plan your performance and manage your behavior to perfection. To err from time to time or fail occasionally, is natural to man. Your personal greatness before God lies in 1) a humble desire and sincere effort to live with a realistic respect for truth, 2) a reasonable fulfillment of your personal needs and wants, and 3) an intelligent concern for the welfare of others. Your inner peace and contentment in this life, depend on a realistic acceptance of the frailties and limitations caused by your unconscious or unintended negative habits. Whether you build a crude hut or a magnificent mansion, you will have made the most of your life if you built what you could with what you had. God will be pleased to dwell within your structure in this life, and to invite you into His eternal dwelling hereafter.

PART FIVE

Re-Assessment and Renewal

AMID the complexities which man finds within himself and in his dealings with others, he might be inclined to simply give up his daily effort to gain a fuller self-possession and a more satisfying self-management. He will fight off this inclination in proportion as he can see a dependable solution. Though every man is limited by his very nature, his limits are broadened in proportion as he can respect himself and see himself respected, loved, and assisted by God. This was precisely the mission of Christ on earth. Through Him, man was so united to God as to be raised above his natural dignity and powers. Though still limited in his supernatural thinking, desires, and efforts, he now has a greater appreciation of his good will and sincere efforts to develop the life-style of Christ within himself. In other words, believing in Christ's loving union with him, man is now disposed to offer a daily effort to be more Christlike, regardless of the limitations and shortcomings in his effort. He really believes that God looks more to his effort than to the results.

He now possesses the peace of Christ through God's supernatural gifts of faith, hope, and love.

27

The Complexities of Human Nature

1 NO MATTER how noble your desires or sincere your efforts, as long as you see your daily behavior as a simple matter of right or wrong and a clear case of black and white, you will constantly be subject to serious misunderstandings of yourself and others. You will often have doubts about yourself and the people with whom you deal. These doubts will arouse insecurity and anxiety in you, and will cause you to be restricted by your mistaken self-defenses. You need to understand your human nature as far as possible, if you are to live with a sense of freedom, spontaneity, and reasonable contentment.

2 Man is not a pure spirit in full possession of himself at all times. Neither is he a mere evolutionary product of the brute beast, totally controlled by blind instincts and rigidly compelled by his spontaneous drives, urges, needs, feelings, and emotions. He is a marvelous combination of both in one composite nature, and his purpose on earth is the balanced fulfillment of his entire being. How far

each individual achieves such a fulfillment, depends on many factors, both natural and supernatural. Though every man has his natural limitations and personal defects, there is something glorious about being human. The more you reflect on the possibilities of human nature, so much the more will you be convinced that man is truly God's masterpiece on earth.

3   Though human nature has many qualities in common with the animal world, it also manifests powers far beyond those of the brute beast. Of all the living creatures on earth, man alone is capable of advancing from the utter helplessness of infancy to a self-determining adulthood. He can view himself with considerable objectivity, and analyze external reality to the point of seeing meaning and purpose in what he observes. He can learn from past human experience, expand his personal knowledge beyond its present boundaries, and change himself for the better within the limits of his nature and circumstances. Man alone can detect the fingerprints of a Master Architect within the intricate order of an ever-evolving creation. Not only is he able to experience the presence of God in the universe, but he can also reach

out to his Maker with an ever-probing intellect and sincere good will. Enlightened and inspired by divine grace, man is disposed and enabled to participate knowingly and willingly in the divine process of creation through an intelligent management of himself and the world around him. Finally, man alone is capable of turning away from His Creator through a conscious and voluntary misuse of the same noble gifts that make him God's masterpiece on earth.

4   In spite of these spiritual powers, man remains quite aware of his constant dependence on the material world around him. For the maintenance of his physical life and general sense of well-being, he needs air, water, food, some measure of material comforts, recreation, rest, and the proper operation and coordination of his bodily functions. His spiritual faculties are always affected in some way when he is beset by hunger, thirst, fatigue, tension, pain, disease, or any other form of excess, frustration, or stress. In short, man's clarity of thought, freedom of self-determination, and management of his unreasoning feelings and spontaneous emotions, are constantly being influenced by the physical conditions of his environment and

the physiological balance of his bodily functions.

5   The influence of your body on your spirit, however, is only part of the complexity of your human nature. Your spirit also plays its part in complicating your daily efforts toward self-possession. It is not only the life-principle of your biological existence, but it also exerts its own proper influence on the orderly functioning of your bodily organs and organ-systems. The spirit does this through your "mind." The mind is the organized totality of your body-spirit interrelation and interaction. By their union and mutual activity, your spirit and body are able to produce your sensations, perceptions, imaginations, dreams, memories, thought-processes, emotions, moods, attitudes, desires, preferences, prejudices, and decisions. Not only does your mind form these activities, but it also stores them and re-activates them when circumstances require it to do so. Your mind is neither your body alone, nor your spirit alone. It is the two together, so intimately interwoven in a vital union, that any joint impression or expression of theirs is experienced by you as one single act of your total self.

6   In spite of the unity of each mental activity

of yours, you know from experience that the workings of your mind can sometimes be quite complicated and confusing. When your spirit expresses its needs, wants, loves, fears and hates, your body registers the physical feelings and mental dispositions corresponding to these expressions of the spirit. In terms of the body, your mental operations and emotional responses involve your senses, nervous system, brain, glands, muscles, organs, and organ-systems. Your face, eyes, voice, breathing, blood pressure, gastro-intestinal tract, and other bodily parts and processes reveal your state of mind even when you are unaware of it yourself. In the complex structure and operations of your brain, many mental activities and their corresponding emotional expressions are formed, interrelated, and associated in such a manner that you are not always sure why you feel as you do, or even understand what you feel about some particular person or situation.

7 Moreover, your body's organic condition and physiological processes can make your mental and emotional behavior not only difficult to comprehend, but also hard to manage on some occasions. For instance, some physical indisposition may incline you

to be ultra-sensitive, impatient, critical, moody, etc. An over-simplified view of your human nature can induce you to blame yourself for "harboring" such feelings, emotions or attitudes, even though these mental operations may involve no deliberate intention or moral consent of yours. Though you may be firmly convinced of this in theory, you may still experience some feelings of self-doubt or guilt. This will usually be due to a mental habit of confusing your feelings and emotions with your rational thinking and free consent.

8   Mental and emotional habits have a material element in them, since the mind is composed partly of the body. This fact makes it harder for you to change your mental and emotional habits than to change your mistaken spiritual ways of thinking or judging. Thus, you may actually correct your erroneous ideas and misjudgments with relative ease through education and study. This does not mean that your emotional views or feelings will change along with your new intellectual convictions. Your old feelings will hold on like a muscle that has been trained wrongly in some sport. It will take you longer to unlearn and relearn than it would take to learn correctly for the first time.

9 As this larger perspective becomes a habit, you will have a fuller understanding of the normality of your nature's complexity and a deeper appreciation of its resistance to change. You will become less inclined to doubt or blame yourself for your unintended negative behavior. You will see your body's material composition, organic structure, and physiological processes as a natural barrier to your spiritual efforts for a fuller self-possession. As you try to assume a greater command over your behavior, you will not expect quick results or perfect achievement. You will have a more realistic appreciation of nature's pace, even with the assistance of God's grace. You will understand that your efforts and progress will require a price of you. If you concentrate your attention primarily on your emotional thinking, you will be overcome with feelings of inadequacy, insecurity, anxiety, or hostility.

10 Enlightened and inspired by divine grace, your spirit will incline you to rise above the level of your unthinking habits. It will also enlarge the scope of your sense of well-being, by helping you view your natural needs and wants in their relation to your total human fulfillment both here and hereafter. With a deep sense of faith and trust in God, together with a realistic grasp of the meaning, purpose, and value of earthly things, your spirit will strive to simplify life as far as this is possible. It will strive first for a soul-satisfying self-possession by reducing your needs to a convenient minimum and respecting these needs in the order of their basic priority. Your spirit will urge you to value first things first in spite of your persistent contrary tendencies and recurring negative emotions. God is less interested in how well you succeed than in how sincerely and persistently you continue to try in spite of imperfect results and complete failures. If you love God and your own greater well-being enough to do this, you can be sure of God's welcome into eternal life.

28

A Realistic Self-Possession

¹AS YOU give more thought to the complexities of your nature, you will find yourself somewhat more understanding and less intolerant of the limitations and shortcomings of your daily behavior. Whatever your conscious intentions, you are constantly being influenced by a number of needs, feelings,

and emotions, both within yourself and within others. In spite of your deliberate efforts to guide your conscious behavior with your natural intelligence and supernatural faith, your nature is spontaneously inclined to maintain its sense of well-being by satisfying your needs, wants, and desires in whatever way seems convenient for the moment. Your sense of well-being can be disturbed on the physical level, mental-emotional level, or spiritual level. Sometimes your disturbance may occur on one of these levels, sometimes on two, and sometimes on all three levels at the same time. Is it any wonder then, that you sometimes find yourself unable to achieve a wise self-management amid your physical tensions, mental confusion, emotional turmoil or moral indecision?

2 A wise self-management can be achieved only by one who is realistically self-possessed. The realistic man tries to live in constant contact with the basic realities, truth, and principles of his earthly existence. He strives for enough knowledge to be reasonably correct in his daily thinking, attitudes, and outlook. He strives for goals and ideals that lie within his powers, and seeks his self-fulfillment with due regard for law and order, and with

reasonable consideration for the feelings and
well-being of others. His vision of life is
broad enough to show him both the advantages and disadvantages in the situations
which he meets each day. In short, he strives
to direct his daily self-management not only
toward his immediate fulfillment, but also
toward his fullest possible well-being both
here and hereafter. He refuses to let his
intellectual convictions and spiritual yearnings be dominated by the unreasoning emotions or moods of each passing hour. Rather,
he tries to follow his deeper insights and
desires in spite of the superficial wants and
frustrations that keep interfering with his
realistic self-possession.

3 Do not be surprised or ashamed if you
feel some reluctance or even hopelessness at
the thought of a planned effort for a fuller
self-possession. These feelings may well be
due to disappointing results in your past
efforts. With a deep appreciation of your
nature's complexity, you will be more realistic,
and therefore more reasonable, in your future
expectations. Like God, you will respect the
good will in your effort rather than condemn
yourself for the unwanted and unintended
defects in your performance. Your self-

possession will never be perfect unless God chooses to grant you a miracle. Barring such a miracle, it is God's will that you be satisfied with reasonable efforts in your daily self-management.

4   In spite of past failures in your efforts for self-renewal, you can still achieve a satisfying growth in self-possession. Your present efforts need not make your daily life any more complex or difficult than it is now. Within the limited time, energies, and opportunities at your disposal, you can: 1) strive for sufficient knowledge of the essential facts of daily human living; 2) center your daily outlook and attitudes around your main purpose in this world; 3) develop a sense of prudence to help you make the best possible decision in your daily problems and conflicts; 4) try to be fair-minded and just in your dealings with others; 5) develop sufficient fortitude to keep you striving for realistic goals and reasonable ideals, in spite of imperfect results or repeated failures in your efforts; and 6) build up enough self-control to direct your unreasoning feelings, wants, and emotions with balance and moderation toward desirable and possible goals.

5   As you can see from these basic principles,

your striving for self-possession is the work of a lifetime. It ends only with death. Why so? Because your feelings and emotions will not always conform to your rational thinking and intelligent judgment. The personality structure and habit-patterns you possess to-day, were developed through years of trying to maintain or protect your sense of well-being. Your deepest drives, urges, needs, and wants are accustomed to being expressed and ful-filled in ways that are now habitual with you. Though you may have a clear intellectual understanding of objective good and evil, you still have to contend with your unreasoning preferences and blind prejudices. To these irrational forces, whatever frustrates or up-sets the sense of well-being is seen or felt as "bad"; and whatever satisfies the sense of well-being is seen or felt as "good." You will never achieve such a degree of self-possession as to be utterly free of this inner conflict. It is the lot of every man on earth to bear his share of this daily burden. Thus, you will always find some room for further growth in your daily self-possession and self-manage-ment. You will persevere in this effort only in proportion as you are able to ac-cept imperfect successes and recurring failures. In that same proportion will you be realistically self-possessed.

6   As you saw in the previous chapter, your inner conflicts occur mainly and mostly within your mind. It is there that your unreasoning emotions, your intellectual convictions, and your moral efforts meet and contend for their own individual fulfillment and well-being. It is in your mind that your sense of well-being is pulled and pushed toward the different levels of your needs, wants, and desires. Which level wins out in each conflict, depends on the respective strength of the habits contending in the conflict of the moment. Even God's grace sometimes depends, in some mysterious way, on the good natural habits you have developed thus far in life. Though you may be struggling to follow your better judgment, you may also find yourself "reluctant" to do so in a particular effort. You may even find yourself positively unwilling to think objectively and act logically in some situations. At such times, your sense of well-being is being dominated by the needs or wants of your mind-body level of life. Your bodily feelings, imagination, and emotions may be so intermingled and intense at the moment, as to make their needs or wants

feel more urgent than the realities, needs, and
desires of your higher spiritual level of life.
7 On these occasions, your spirit is torn
between its strong sense appetites and emotions, and its intellectual convictions and
higher aspirations. Though grace is always
at your disposal, the daily human struggle for
self-possession is not always an easy one. The
supernatural habits of your spirit were infused into you through baptism and divine
grace. They grow through your application in
daily life. At times these divine gifts may not
have been practiced enough to compete with
the more experienced natural habits of your
body-mind level of life. Thus, it is possible
for you to want to follow your intelligent
desires, and still surrender to your more
earthly needs and wants of the moment. Like
Saint Paul, you too may sometimes feel or do
what you do not approve of, or be unable to
achieve what your spirit sincerely desires. In
spite of all this, you can still plan and strive
for a further growth in your self-possession
and self-management.
8 Your self-possession will be realistic in
so far as you strive to direct your feelings,
needs, wants, and emotions with whatever
correct knowledge, understanding, and de-

termination you have at present. Toward what goals are you to direct them? Direct them toward their natural goals in so far as these goals fit into the overall purpose of your personal life. Whatever makes sense in your earthly behavior, also makes sense with God. Just as extremes and disorder violate the requirements of nature, so too do they violate the plan of God in His creation. Thus, you must learn to see your natural life and your religious principles and beliefs as joint elements of your total existence. Nature and grace are like the right and left hand of God, uniting your earthly fulfillment with your eternal glory. Life does not end with the death of the body. It is merely changed into its most perfect form. Only then will your self-possession be completely "sanctified in truth."

9 Where to begin? Begin with here and now. Try to focus your thinking on the most basic facts of life and the most central truths of God's revelation to man. In His creation, God has involved Himself with you in a very personal way. This involvement is more intimate than that between you and the air you breathe or the food you eat. Whatever your feelings or thoughts in this matter, you cannot change this fact that God has joined Himself

to you through His constant creative presence and sustaining support in everything you experience within and around you. Moreover, in His plan of redemption, God put most of the burden, not on you, but upon His willing and self-giving Son. Through His personal life, Jesus offered His Father a worship and self-dedication that you could never attain by yourself. He took your place, not to make you feel guilty or unworthy, but that you might accept the worth and innocence He earned by taking your place. Your faith in Him is to shine forth in your daily way of life. You do this not by going out of your way to be "religious," but by living each day in the light of reason with the knowledge of divine revelation and the strength of Christ's redeeming grace.

10 Because God respects reality and truth, He does not expect your self-renewal to be any better than "normal in view of your personal history." In other words, God expects your old undesirable habits to recur in spite of your best intentions and sincerest efforts for a satisfactory self-renewal. To God the word "satisfactory" may mean not so much "how well or how quickly you succeed," but how repeatedly you renew your

effort after each failure or imperfect achievement. It's what you can achieve today, with all its flaws and deficiencies, that counts with God and reasonable men. Your self-possession is no less praiseworthy because of your unwanted distractions, unintended failures, and recurring negative habits. Be realistic enough to expect old habits to repeat themselves for some time to come, and refuse to abandon your intelligent ideals and reasonable goals. This is what it means to be realistic. It means facing life as is, and trying to build with the material at hand.

11 As your spirit absorbs the heavenly message of God's central place in your daily life, you will gradually see your earthly life in a broader, more inspiring perspective. In your daily experiences, your point of reference will not be "only here and now," but "both here and hereafter, both now and forever." This new orientation will help you evaluate things on the basis of your "total being." Just as you would not leap into the path of an on-coming train to salvage a wind-blown dollar bill, so too, you will refuse to over-estimate or under-estimate the people, things, and situations which are an integral part of your earthly life.

12 It cannot be stressed too often that God

looks more to your effort than to the results of these efforts. His everyday graces will not bring you a sudden, complete development, but a gradual, healthy growth based on: 1) your faith in your own good will, as well as in God's personal concern about you; 2) your ability to keep working patiently toward your gradual development, no matter how slow the pace or imperfect the visible results; and 3) your willingness to show God a loyalty of persevering effort if that is all you can achieve. God's daily graces will elevate and strengthen your nature in its persistent efforts to live in accordance with right reason and God's plan of creation and redemption. You can best work toward this goal by impressing the essential realities, truths, and principles of life on your mind and spirit. Through daily doses of reading, reflection, sacraments and a growing appreciation, you can slowly re-orient your sense of well-being toward its fullest satisfaction and highest fulfillment. With time, experience, and growth, your self-possession and self-management will face less conflicts and a greater integration, because your sense of well-being will have come into a more meaningful contact with the higher values in your life.

29
Man's Need of Faith

1 IN THE Book of Proverbs we read: "Though the virtuous man falls seven times a day, he stands up again." (Prov. 24: 16) We tend to think of virtue as a "freedom from weakness." Yet, in these inspired words of Holy Scripture the virtuous man is described as one who has the faith and courage to get up and try again after having failed. Too many people see virtue only in its perfect performance. To them, the only true virtue is the achieved power to overcome weakness. However, it often requires great virtue to work toward a worthy goal with a realistic desire to do as well as possible, even though one knows that the results will be far from perfect. One reason why people shy away from most forms of self-discipline, is their inability to tolerate partial success. If they make a resolution, they expect to fulfill it at once and to perfection. Blessed is he who is realistic enough to: 1) strive for whatever success he can achieve, and 2) accept unwanted limitations or occasional failures as part of his total effort.

2 Moreover, virtue is not restricted ex-

clusively to the religious or supernatural level of human behavior. There are also natural virtues. They are good habits acquired through the frequent repetition of well-motivated acts. This repetition fulfills one's felt needs or wants so well, as to make the performance of morally good acts easy. Thus, both natural virtues and supernatural virtues are principles of action. They differ, however, in three respects: 1) *In their origin:* Natural virtues are acquired by the satisfying repetition of the same acts. Supernatural virtues are infused into the human spirit together with sanctifying grace. 2) *In their manner of operation:* The natural virtues, through their frequent desired repetition of the same acts, give one a facility of producing the acts readily and with a sense of pleasure. The supernatural virtues give man the "power" to produce good supernatural acts together with a certain "tendency" toward producing these acts; but man is still obliged to develop his own facility through voluntary practice. 3) *In their purpose:* Natural virtues seek man's natural well-being, and thereby direct him toward the God of Nature, i.e., God in His natural gifts here on earth. Supernatural virtue seeks man's total well-being, both natural and supernatural, and thereby directs man toward the God of Revelation, with His "Good News" of divine love, redemption, adoption, and sanctification in this earthly life together with an expectation of resurrection into eternal life.

3   Thus, while all virtues look to man's fufillment, natural virtues seek it here and now, whereas supernatural virtues look to man's fulfillment both here and hereafter, now and forever. When one's temporal well-being is in conflict with his eternal well-being, his supernatural virtues incline him to prefer his most complete and most enduring fulfillment. With the help of God's grace and sufficient practice, any man can improve his self-possession and self-management better than he ever could through natural habits alone. In other words, God's supernatural help brings you a greater degree of integration between your grace-inspired thinking and your natural reason, and also between your natural emotional leanings and your grace-supported choices. There will always be some confusion and conflict between your rational judgments and your unthinking inclinations; however, this inner division and weakness need not surprise you nor burden you with

shame, self-blame, or guilt-feelings. Your grace-supported intelligence and good will can help you understand and accept this "natural" condition of every man on earth. In some of your needs and wants you can expect only a limited fulfillment, due to your inherited nature, past history, and present established habits of body, mind, and spirit. With this enlarged perspective of life, you will refuse to strain anxiously for perfect achievement or surrender hopelessly to discouragement in your daily efforts for self-renewal.

4   The first virtue necessary for achieving a satisfactory performance in your daily routine, is the virtue of faith. Even the avowed atheist needs to exercise some kind of faith, whether it be faith in himself, or in other people, or in some object or situation in which he trusts for his desired fulfillment. After all, every man is inadequate to help himself in all his needs and wants. He needs the assistance and cooperation of others in a number of ways. He therefore has no choice but to believe or trust that his desires and needs will be fulfilled as well as can be expected. In proportion as you doubt either yourself or others, you will be burdened with insecurity and troubled by anxiety. The weaker your

faith in the real facts of your personal situation, the harder you will find it to maintain your self-possession. Your intelligence will be limited by your imagination, and your imagination will be controlled by your anxieties and fears. You will be unable to judge the situation with a reasonable objectivity. Your self-management will be dictated by your unreasoning mind and unthinking emotions. In short, in proportion as you cannot believe and trust yourself, others, God, or life itself, you are the slave of your nature's blind drives and self-destructive urges. You need faith if you are to avoid or alleviate this unhealthy development within yourself.

5 Fortunately, most people are disposed to exercise some measure of faith in their daily life. This faith consists in some kind of willingness and ability to believe, trust, or rely on oneself, others, or some object in one's daily efforts for his necessary achievements and fulfillment. This faith may be natural or supernatural. Natural faith proceeds from one's natural feelings and sentiments, or from his educated moral convictions. Supernatural faith consists of one's grace-inspired readiness to accept certain truths and facts on the authority of God Himself.

Moreover one's faith is mature in so far as it helps him: 1) to face reality, 2) to strive to understand life's meaning and its manner of fulfillment, and 3) to endeavor to live in accordance with his own reasonable needs and wants with due regard for the reasonable needs and wants of others. Faith is immature if its main purpose is solely to help one escape the necessary burdens of life or avoid the unpleasant requirements of right order.

6   Long before you exercised any intellectual, moral, supernatural faith, you had already lived a number of years depending on the material, emotional, and moral support of your parents. In your utter dependency, you relied on their constant assistance. In your helplessness, you saw your elders as all-knowing and all-powerful in those matters that concerned your well-being. You found security in conforming to their wishes and expectations. You felt confident or doubtful in proportion as you did or did not feel able and disposed to follow their requirements. Your need to feel secure and free of anxiety, inclined you to adopt the general attitudes and standards of behavior which your parents demanded of you. In sheer necessity, you tended to conform to their views and regula-

tions. Only by conforming could you gain the
acceptance and approval that you needed for
the preservation of your sense of security
and well-being.

7 In their sincerity and good will, your
parents, guardians and tutors cared for you
and trained you not only with the knowledge
and experience which they had acquired
through life, but also with the dispositions,
sentiments and attitudes with which they
interpreted this knowledge and experience.
They simply could not present life and its
fundamental principles to you without also
transmitting their personal emotional leanings on each particular subject. Consequently,
they taught you not only to believe what they
believed, but also to feel somewhat as they
themselves felt about these beliefs. In some
limited degree, they were sharing their inner
emotional experience with you. How you
responded to this sharing, depended on how
it affected your sense of well-being. You accepted whatever bolstered it, and rejected
whatever seemed too painful or difficult. Most
of your rejections or rebellions were either
partially or totally repressed, i.e., immediately disguised or hidden from your direct
awareness. Such repressions eventually be-

came so swift and automatic as to occur without your least notice.

8 In his own particular manner, every child does his share of rebelling against some of the demands and expectations of his elders. Most children, however, do more complying than rebelling. In proportion as a child feels his inadequacy and dependence on his parents and elders, he also feels a need to have their good will and approval. He feels a close identity with them, a feeling that he belongs to them, and they to him. This dependence and identification incline him to see life through the attitudes and outlook of these significant adults. Sometimes consciously and sometimes unconsciously, the child tends to adopt its parents' viewpoint on many subjects. Their ideas of "good" and "bad", "right" and "wrong", are impressed on him all through his formative years. The basic thinking of parents and other significant elders is absorbed morning, noon and night by the growing child. The will, wishes and general attitudes of these elders constitute a large part of the emotional atmosphere in which the child lives and develops his own particular needs, wants, and habits. Even the "disobedient" child feels some insecur-

ity, guilt, or fear of punishment for his deviations from his expected behavior.

9   So well are the thinking and attitudes of parents and elders impressed on the growing child that he identifies their will and wishes with his own security and sense of well-being. Even in later years, when his intellectual and moral judgment has developed, he never quite outgrows some of this identification. As an adult, he still experiences some vague uneasiness or guilt-feeling when he violates what he "feels" is right or performs what he "feels" is wrong. This tendency to live by one's early emotional habits, is deeply rooted in the mind. Even those who abandon their earlier beliefs and external practices, never fully emancipate themselves from their childhood emotional development. They "feel" free only as long as they can remain distracted from people, things, or situations which remind them of their past. When reminded or in danger of being reminded, they may manifest some uneasiness or hostility. They need this hostility to protect themselves from old intolerable feelings of inadequacy, insecurity, and anxiety. They profess to "believe differently from the past," but they find it hard to remain totally undisturbed when

their new "faith" comes face to face with reminders of their early-life faith.

10   Your early-life faith was not an intellectual consent as to whether or not to believe in your parents and other significant elders. It was a belief arising from your utter dependence on these adults. Out of this dependence there arose also an emotional demand within you, a demand that you conform to the expectations and requirements of these adults. This conformity would bring you their approval plus your own fulfillment and well-being. So closely identified was this conformity and your well-being that you could hardly distinguish which was which. Consequently your inner emotional demand for this conformity acted as a "warning signal" whenever you felt inclined to act contrary to the wishes of your parents or significant elders. It also acted as a "critic" whenever you fell short of their desires. It disturbed your sense of well-being whenever you sensed the possibility of disapproval or punishment for your contrary behavior. This emotional demand was not free and voluntary within you. Being so closely allied with your sense of well-being, it arose spontaneously and independently of your contrary wants or desires. In short, it

acted as a sort of "superior self," a super-ego whose function it was to direct your behavior "aright." This super-ego demanded that you avoid any sense of failure, guilt, or fear of punishment.

11   The super-ego does not die in later life. It is so deeply rooted in the mind that it influences one's emotional thinking in spite of his better judgment. It continues to function because it is intimately involved with man's sense of well-being and self-preservation. Though your super-ego be strong, moderate or weak, it will continue to present some obstacles to your sincere efforts for a fuller, firmer and more realistic faith in yourself, in those with whom you deal and in God. In its own vague or indirect ways, it inclines you to compare what you see in yourself (your self-image) with what you feel you "should" or "must" be, (your self-ideal). When aroused, your super-ego brings some sense of doubt or guilt either about 1) what you are, 2) what you are not, or 3) what you should be. These negative feelings weaken your faith in yourself, make you unsure of others, and doubtful of God's love or concern about you.

12   The "reasoning process" of the super-ego goes somewhat like this: "Whatever you

do, you must do it well, so well that there will
be no doubts or regrets about it. If you do it
perfectly, you will have no reason to doubt
yourself. You will not have to calculate
whether you could have done better, or why
you did not do better. If you do anything
imperfectly, you are guilty of disturbing your
sense of well-being with feelings of insecurity
and anxiety. You must therefore establish a
perfect self-ideal; and what is more, you
must strive to achieve that ideal without
making excuses for yourself. Stop pampering
yourself and begin at last to prove your
sincerity! Anything short of this ideal is
nothing!" The above line of thinking comes
to most people in less clear or less definite
concepts. Most of this process lies hidden
beneath and beyond your direct awareness.
All that you may feel is some measure of
disappointment with yourself with an indefinable sense of uneasiness, when things do
not go as you had planned or hoped.

13 The super-ego is not interested in
"thinking with the facts." As it did in childhood, it still lives and thrives strictly on
imagination, emotions, and feelings. It looks
only to the flaws in your performance. It
blames you for your shortcomings, without

giving any consideration to the circumstances of the situation. It has only two ratings, namely, one hundred percent and zero. It induces people to strain either from an anxious eagerness for success or from a fear of failure. The super-ego gradually undermines one's faith in himself. This lack of self-assurance leads to insecurity with other people and guilt-feelings with God. The super-ego is one of the worst enemies of emotional contentment and spiritual peace. Slowly but steadily, it draws some people ever closer to a weakening of their supernatural faith and an abandonment of their religious practices.

14 Some people mistake their super-ego for their conscience. As long as this misunderstanding persists, these people are exposed to many unnecessary difficulties in their religious practices. They may feel obliged to repeat a prayer until they have recited it without a single distraction. Others may find themselves torn between genuine need for rest or recreation, and a strong emotional doubt as to whether they should spend that time doing something "more profitable" or "more meritorious." This impossible tyranny of the super-ego induces some to diminish their interest in religion, and others to aban-

don altogether every religious practice, even the sacraments. From this you may see how the super-ego can weaken your faith if given a chance. It can do this by inducing you to live more on your emotions, imagination, and feelings than on a dependable knowledge and understanding of human nature and divine revelation. A number of people live by the limited knowledge they acquired in childhood. They have never brought their knowledge up to date. Consequently, their true conscience is often unequipped to rectify the erroneous thinking process of the super-ego. They see hardships flowing from further knowledge and obligations. Their lack of knowledge also inclines them to neglect the sacraments. They therefore also lack some of the graces needed to restrain their super-ego when it threatens to break down their good will or incline them to foster ideas and practices which are dangerous to their best interests.

15 When true conscience is adequately informed and sufficiently at peace to make a balanced moral judgment, it is also able to act as a counterbalance to the blind, unthinking urges of the super-ego. True conscience is able to distinguish honest mistakes and

unintended weaknesses from deliberate faults and real bad will. Even in doubt, the true conscience acknowledges the doubt, and tries to establish some reasonable principle of action for the moment, whereas the super-ego keeps the mind reeling from one doubt to another. While the super-ego thrives on the rigid emotional thinking of early life, the true conscience is able to advance in knowledge, accept new ideas, and adjust to the intelligible changing customs of later generations.

16 The real human conscience is man's practical intellect, i.e., his spiritual faculty by which he can judge the conformity of his behavior to the moral requirements of his nature as a whole. It is concerned with the objective orderliness of one's freely chosen conduct. True conscience bases its judgment on the very nature of things. It takes into account all the details related to one's spontaneous behavior, his self-possession, and his deliberate self-management in any particular situation. Like a well-functioning bodily organ, a well balanced conscience brings you a sense of well-being when your behavior is orderly, and a sense of insecurity or anxiety when your conduct is out of line with right reason. Moreover, true con-

science brings a sense of satisfaction and self-contentment when you have acted well. Your faith will remain strong as long as your conscience is at peace. Your faith can then grow in vision, vitality, and spiritual contentment.

17   Just as it took years to develop the mental and emotional habits by which you live your present daily life, so too will it require some amount of time and persevering effort to improve your faith, both natural and supernatural. Without faith on both levels of life, you will have only a partial perspective and a diminished spontaneity and enthusiasm in your self-management. Though old mental and emotional habits will persist, faith in your ultimate victory will keep you just as persistent against them. Faith will prevent you from surrendering to guilt feelings or discouragement when you have your inevitable setbacks. In the face of recurring self-doubts, at least express an act of faith in your desire to continue working toward whatever self-renewal you can achieve without going to unwise extremes.

18   How can you enrich your daily life with a strong natural and supernatural faith? How can you best undo the negative mental and emotional habits of years? As long as these

habits dominate your behavior, you will find yourself frustrated, discouraged, disinterested or disillusioned. Your first step toward strengthening your faith in yourself, other people and God, may well be the adopting of a "scientific attitude" toward "Project Self-Renewal." Such an attitude will help you concentrate more on the facts as they really are, than on the facts as they "might have been" or "should be." Only when you strive to put more faith in objective reality as far as it is attainable, and less faith in your established negative feelings and attitudes—only then can you say, "Now I have really begun!" If this beginning is genuine, you will be prepared to renew your faith and continue trying with each recurring failure.

19 Your first impressions of God were developed from the religious thinking and feelings of your parents, tutors, and other significant individuals involved in your life. As a growing child, you saw God as loving or demanding, warmly merciful or coldly just, broadly understanding or rigidly critical. Whatever your impression, it was composed of many ingredients, such as the knowledge, experience, emotions, and graces of others, plus your own knowledge, experience, emo-

tions and graces. Moreover, your impression of God was also constructed from the unspoken attitudes and behavior of these people, in regard to religion, and morality. Though you have forgotten most of your early-life experiences, their negative effects on your sense of well-being are stored in the unconscious levels of your mind. Within your grasp you have only the definite thoughts, attitudes, and practices whereby you now express your religious faith. Make good use of these in so far as they are positive and helpful. In so far as they are negative and harmful, strive to eliminate or modify them with a fuller knowledge, deeper understanding, and a persevering effort to build new attitudes and goals.

20 Though man ought to see himself as a child of God, he is not expected to act childishly in his encounters with God. God would have you face Him with an honest and grateful acknowledgement of your utter dependence on Him. On the other hand, He would also have you show a healthy self-respect for the natural and supernatural gifts which He has bestowed on you. He would prefer that you trust Him through your supernatural faith than fear Him through your natural doubts and insecurity. You are God's child

not merely by His having created you, but
also by His having sent His divine Son to
raise you to a supernatural state of redemption and adoption. Finally, God has raised
you up to a supernatural level of union with
Him through the sanctifying gifts of the
Holy Spirit.

21 God's sanctifying gifts are not external
additions to your natural gifts. They are infused into your natural faculties and powers,
somewhat as the spirit dwells and functions
in the body, and together with the body forms
one composite individual being. The union of
your natural self with God's supernatural
graces does not change your daily life in its
external appearances. You still have your
daily chores to perform, your human problems
to solve, and your personal gifts and talents
to use and enjoy in the variety of situations
that come your way. The difference lies in
the fact that you act with supernatural grace
joined to your natural powers. Supernatural
faith enlarges your natural perspective. Supernatural hope broadens, elevates, and
strengthens your personal motivations. Supernatural love moves you to give of yourself to
God in the persons and things involved in
your daily activities.

22 Thus, God's gift of supernatural faith is intended to inspire you with a filial trust and confidence in His fatherly concern for you. This gift militates against your natural emotionally-induced doubts arising from your past negative experiences. True, God expects an honest sorrow for real sins, but He also expects you to leave your guilt at His feet once you have made amends. Instead of looking backward to re-examine any possible flaw in your reparation for past sins, God would have you look forward with positive goals and with a reasonable faith in the future. Let the "unprofitable" past be buried under a "profitable" present. In what does this profit consist? It consists in living each day with a readiness to make the most of it and with a reasonable enjoyment. Just live this day and leave your yesterdays and tomorrows in the hands of God. The fact that you cannot understand the hardships and disappointments that happen to you or others, does not justify your doubting the goodness, wisdom, or existence of God. True, such doubts may not be due to bad will, but to natural habits developed from past emotional experiences. Sometimes all that you can do with them is tolerate them. Even though your "feelings" create doubts and fears in you, insist on "believing" that they are not imputable to you as long as you do not "want" them.

23   Much as you may desire to acquire the supernatural vision and perspective presented here, you will soon find that such an acquisition is not achieved in a day. Your well-entrenched natural habits of mind and body will gradually slow down the eager new trends of your spirit. Your grace-enlightened thinking will still be interrupted by your negative "feelings," your unwanted imaginings or emotions, and your blind prejudices or narrow preferences. Your grace-inspired desires and efforts will still have to contend with your natural limitations, the recurring demands of long-standing habits, and the misguided urgings of your natural sense of well-being. Though your spirit may prefer to strive for a greater self-possession, your physical and emotional needs and wants will continue to distract your intelligence and weaken your spirit's efforts for a greater at-home-ness with God. In spite of your supernatural trust in God, you will still be tempted by your doubts and discouragements to reduce or abandon your efforts for a fuller perspective and a steadier self-management in your daily behavior.

24 Thus, besides faith in God's fatherly interest and concern, you also need a good dose of faith in your own good will and eventual success in achieving a notable degree of self-renewal. You need to believe that you are worth the effort. You also need to believe that your contrary inclinations and feelings are not necessarily a proof of bad will. You will be less confused by your self-doubts if you see them for what they are, namely, habits stemming from your past experiences, especially the experiences of early life. It was then that you were most inadequate to help yourself and most in need of others. Your dependency aroused insecurity and anxiety many times in those years of basic formation. In varying degrees, every man has a lasting sensitivity to the numberless possibilities of recurring insecurity and anxiety. In short, for all your knowledge, experience, and graces, you walk each day the well-known path of established habits and habit-systems, whereby you seek to maintain a balanced sense of well-being. Since your success depends partly on other people and partly on God, your self-confidence is constantly faced with some uncertainty or doubt. You cannot always predict how others will receive your behavior,

nor will you always "feel sure" how God views your performance. Consequently you cannot live totally free of some insecurity and anxiety.

25 In His own mysterious way, God offers His supernatural gift of faith to every man of good will. This gift does not usually operate independently of your natural habits and limitations. Thus, your supernatural desire to express confidence in God's care and providence, may be hindered or weakened by your natural self-doubts or even by an unconscious natural fear of rejection. Though these contrary tendencies may occur simultaneously within you, you may not realize that they occur on different levels of your thinking and volition. Your expression of supernatural faith occurs on the higher level of abstract thought, rational judgment and moral choice, enlightened and inspired by divine grace. On the physical-emotional-imagination level of your behavior, you experience insecurity, doubts, and anxiety, plus your natural urge to calm your feelings by following your emotional thinking. This lower level of behavior is more closely involved with your complex mind-body interaction of organs, nervous systems, and

mental-emotional needs and wants. On occasion these two different levels of thinking and acting become so intertwined as to make you unsure as to which level is predominant at the moment. Your self-doubt at such times is very understandable.

26 Another source of self-doubt may be the fact that your physical and emotional needs and wants are often felt more strongly and intensely than your less material goals and desires. Do not be surprised at this. Your unspiritual inclinations and wants have had much more practice than your spiritual needs, desires, and intentions. For the first dozen years of life, man lives predominantly on his physical-fantasy-emotional level of awareness and wants. Your intellectual and moral powers developed more slowly on their spiritual level of abstract, logical, grace-enlightened thought and rational, deliberate, grace-supported choice. Even with God's grace, your higher level of thinking and choosing continues to feel some influence from your lower level of needs and wants. Even Jesus felt this division within His human nature during His temptations in the desert and in His agony in the Garden of Olives. Nevertheless, this experience of inner

division and conflict can sometimes create serious doubts about yourself, other people, or God.

27 This division within your human nature is natural and normal to every man. If you can become "scientifically-minded" enough to accept this fact, not only in theory, but also in practice, you will gradually enjoy an ever greater self-possession. You will be more disposed to accept some inevitable self-doubts without becoming unduly disturbed. You will not waste too much time trying to make a "sure" decision as to your guilt or innocence. If you cannot make a moral estimate of the doubt-causing situation within a reasonable time, leave it in the understanding hands of God. Life is too precious to waste on endless efforts to "make absolutely sure." Let your faith in God's wisdom and goodness prove itself on these occasions. Relying on God's gift of supernatural faith and trust, you will enjoy a greater mental clarity and emotional balance. Being at peace with God, you will also have more peace with yourself and with those around you. Though some inner echoes of doubt may still be heard, put your trust in God, and rest assured that He will not fail you. He really wants you to be adult

enough to respect your honest opinion in spite of the possibilities of your being mistaken.

28 Your faith in your fellowmen is not always easy to maintain. Every man has his own inner needs and wants, his own problems, frustrations, and conflicts, and the strong preferences and prejudices of his particular sense of well-being. Your interpersonal problem is largely one of trying to balance your own needs and wants with those of others. Since human nature is functioning on both sides of every interpersonal communication, some measure of misunderstandings and some occasional friction may be expected. All that you can do is to go along trying to be considerate and respectful of others, without losing due consideration and respect for your own reasonable needs and wants. You will achieve this balance in proportion as you learn to see Christ in your fellowman. Jesus did say that He would personally thank you for any assistance and self-giving that you might offer to others. At the last judgment He will publicly declare before all mankind: "You did it to me." (Matt. 25: 31-46) The greater your faith in the "Good News" of Christ, the bigger a person will you be in your dealings with others. Do not feel obliged to go to

extremes in this self-giving for Christ. Simply do what you can in the occasions that arise naturally in your daily routine.

29 How well you respond to God's invitation to a closer friendship with Him through His divine Son, depends partly on the habits that prevail most in your physical, mental, and spiritual needs. If given a chance, God's graces will work wonders in you; but do not make the mistake of demanding more of yourself than God Himself asks. Some of your undesirable habits will continue to recur many times and in many different disguises. Look on your new effort as a lifetime project and look upon God as your very closest partner in this project. He does not want to add to your present burdens and problems. He simply wishes to give you the encouragement of knowing that He is with you and for you. He will not increase your obligations above those which you already have as a human being redeemed by His divine Son. In short, God wishes to help you live your life with a greater fulfillment in reality and a deeper satisfaction in truth.

30 Your peace and friendship with God lies in a fuller knowledge of your human nature and a deeper understanding of Him. You

need to believe in Him, not as a strange being existing somehow somewhere, but as a warmly concerned Father, a self-giving Brother, and an ever-helpful and accompanying Spirit. When the apostle Phillip asked Jesus to show them His Father, Jesus answered, "To have seen me, is to have seen the Father also." (John 14:9) The more you are impressed by God's personal concern for you, the more will you also be impressed by the dignity and worth He has bestowed on you personally. In spreading His "Good News," Jesus pointed out the fatherly providence with which His Father constantly watches over you. (Matt. 6:25-34) Jesus Himself would not even exclude children from His personal encounter.(Matt. 19:13-14) When accused of being the friend of sinners, Jesus stressed His personal love for them as individuals. (Luke 15:4-7) He declared that no man is too small or worthless for God's personal concern. (Luke 15:8-10) The limitless love of God for His erring children was demonstrated in the breath-taking story of the prodigal son. (Luke 15:11-32)

31 Do not be surprised if you meet some people who refuse, in word or fact, to draw closer to God. Their established mental and

emotional habits prevent them somehow. How much each person is to blame for his refusal, only God can say. Some of these people turn away from God because they are doubtful about their ability to meet the requirements of a closer friendship with Him. Others expect to feel intolerable feelings of unworthiness, guilt or fear of punishment in a closer contact with God and religion. Then there are those who are afraid that they may feel too confined or restricted by the rules and regulations imposed on them by religious obligations. Controlled by such negative mental and emotional habits, a number of people see every religious effort at renewal as a mere repetition of unpleasant past experience. They find it hard to believe that God really is as Jesus described His Father.

32   God does not expect the impossible of any man. He asks only that each individual do what he honestly can to live in accordance with the principles of truth, justice, and personal honesty with himself. Where human powers fail, God will somehow supply further supernatural assistance. To those who feel that it is too late to begin again, Jesus presents His personal example. He accepted the last-hour petition of the dying thief on the

cross. (Luke 23:43) To those who think that a new commitment to Christ would require too much "catching up," Christ presents His parable of the workers in the vineyard. (Matt. 20:1-16) The person who feels that he has sinned too much to change his ways, might do well to reflect on Christ's visit to the home of Zacchaeus the tax collector. (Luke 19:1-10) The divine understanding and personal love of Jesus toward sinners, defies all description in the Gospel account of the woman taken in sin. (John 8:3-11)

33 The more you become impressed by Christ's efforts to convince you of His personal friendship and concern for you, the more will you be eager to foster your supernatural gift of faith. As faith grows in your spirit, you will learn to judge your personal worth not so much by what you have done for God, but by what God has done for you. St. John tells us: "God loved the world so much that He gave his only Son, so that everyone who believes in him may not be lost, but may have eternal life." (John 3:16) Christ is the main source of your personal worth. Though you may not feel it, He has given you a value and dignity that raises you above all earthly standards. Unfortunately,

your natural lack of faith in yourself tends to weaken your grace-inspired desire to believe in this supernatural worth bestowed on you through the sacrament of baptism.

34 God's supernatural grace does not free you from all the limitations of your human nature. Even in the state of grace, you are still a member of the human race. Therefore your negative emotional habits and your unthinking drives and inclinations will continue to make themselves felt in spite of your highest desires and noblest efforts for self-renewal. You will still be subject to feelings of inadequacy, insecurity, and anxiety, together with their undesirable consequences. At the same time, however, you do not cease being a man of faith, as long as you hold on to your desire to believe in the "Good News" of Christ. Whatever your passing natural rebellions against God, you will also have your moments of dawning hope and budding supernatural desires. As long as God has even this tiny thread to hold on to, you may rest assured that He will not lose a single opportunity to give you a reminding tug.

35 Whatever your natural doubts or fears, this much is certain: The man who goes on trying to live by his gift of supernatural faith, is credited by God with believing, regardless of his unwanted failures. A skirmish is not a battle, and a battle is not a war. Your earthly campaign for self-renewal is a life-long war for an eternal victory. Your search for an all-satisfying fulfillment is sure of success, as long as you strive to live by your supernatural faith. God did not create you to lose you, nor did He send His divine Son to die for you in vain. It is not necessarily how much visible progress you make in your daily efforts at self-renewal, that shows how great your supernatural faith is. Your best proof of faith may be the fact that you stubbornly refuse to stop trying. When you fall into some weakness or even into a momentary lull in your efforts, your faith may show itself in a desire to begin again. It takes a far stronger faith to begin again and again amid recurring failures, than to continue trying amid increasing successes.

30
Advantages of Hope in Daily Life

1 AS YOU saw in the preceding chapter, the virtue of faith is a basic requirement for a reasonable human fulfillment in this earthly life and for the grander fulfillment promised by God through His divine Son. Every man lives by some kind of faith, whether natural or supernatural or both. Everyone believes in some realities, truths, and principles on which he relies for his fulfillment and contentment. The principal problem of faith is the problem of having sufficient objective reality and essential truth on which to base one's faith. No man can knowingly live a lie or lead a life built on make-believe, without feeling some kind of insecurity and anxiety. His mind may resort to some unconscious mental mechanism to protect its sense of well-being. However, even then, one may still feel some vague uneasiness.

2 Your supernatural faith is a direct gift of God. This gift inclines you to believe in His divine message of creation, redemption, and sanctification. This gift, however, does not work in you without your personal cooperation. Your religious faith needs to be exer-

cised in your everyday life. In His parable of the sower in the field, Jesus showed how the word of God falls on a variety of internal dispositions and external situations which can help or hinder God's influence on your spirit. (Matt. 13:4-9, 18-25) True, God's grace, i.e., His influence on your spirit, is not always felt as it works within you. Jesus said that it can operate as imperceptibly as yeast that ferments dough for baking. (Matt. 13:33)

3 From the preceding parables, you can see that your growth in supernatural grace, i.e., supernatural union with God and cooperation with His inspirations, is not always something that you can measure or evaluate. God's influence on your spirit works in a mysterious manner, i.e., a manner that is not always conscious or understandable. Though you may not feel it, this divine influence extends your inner vision of life beyond your natural boundaries. It also increases your religious desires and moral powers beyond their natural limits. God's supernatural influence on you, works so closely with your natural faculties, that you cannot always be sure where nature ends and God's grace begins within your daily self-management.

4 In spite of all that has just been said, your natural tendency to doubt yourself will sometimes arouse some apprehension about your possible rejection by God. Most people experience occasional misgivings about themselves. They do not always feel so sure that they are performing as well as they might. Though their faith in God's love and understanding may be quite strong, they may feel some uneasiness about whether they themselves have shown enough gratitude or co-operation to deserve God's continued approval. Amid such misgivings, these people stand in need of another virtue, a virtue which will bolster their faith when it weakens or becomes too negative. They need this virtue to help them reaffirm their good will and to inspire them to continue their daily effort for a greater confidence in themselves and a closer friendship with God. The virtue that can achieve all this and more, is the virtue of hope.

5 Hope is needed by every man, whether he lives on a purely natural plane or on the higher and broader plane of religious faith. Like supernatural faith, religious hope is infused directly by God into the human spirit at the same time when he raises the spirit up to a supernatural union with Him. This union with God is called the "state of grace." It is not a momentary state, but an abiding one. It is not static, but dynamic. It can grow or decline somewhat like the life of the body. A man who does not observe the ordinary rules of physical hygiene endangers his bodily health. So too, one who does not foster his state of union with God by an active practice of faith and hope, runs the risk of diminishing the effects of God's influence on his daily attitudes, disposition, judgment, and self-management.

6 A strong supernatural hope inclines you to view life with positive attitudes and a broader perspective. It reminds you that God does not think like mere men. Hope disposes your spirit to believe that God looks more to the effort than to the results. It also helps you to believe that God does not expect you to strain beyond your physical, mental, emotional, or spiritual endurance. Hope inclines the spirit to make frequent acts of faith in God's nearness, trust in His constant assistance, and confidence in His personal concern and fatherly love. Supernatural hope fosters intelligent and orderly desires for self-fulfillment both here and hereafter.

7 Do not be surprised when your negative habits of feeling, imagining, thinking, and wanting resist the positive urgings of supernatural faith and hope. When this occurs your divine gift of hope will incline you to oppose these contrary tendencies with a stubborn confidence in Christ's "Good News" of redemption and sanctification. Your negative tendencies are not always unreasonable. Sometimes they make sense and should be followed. For instance, there are times when you are justified in resenting some injustice, or in disagreeing with others on some issue or idea. In such instances, your supernatural hope will help you moderate your negative responses within proper limits. Moreover, hope helps you keep your eye on God's constant assistance, and this awareness inclines you to avoid foolish extremes in your conscious behavior.

8 When your negative behavior occurs without forewarning or deliberation on your part, it is hope that prevents you from blaming yourself without sufficient reason. Some people are so afraid of self-deceit that they feel safer in accusing themselves than in making an honest judgment of innocence or at least of reasonable doubt. At such times their

super-ego is opposing their sincere effort to
think with their conscience. Beware of needing advice or encouragement in every doubtful situation. Through the virtue of hope, God
encourages you to act as captain of your own
self-management. Such a captaincy often involves some risk of possible error. God will
never blame you for making an honest mistake in your sincere effort to assume responsibility for your own judgment. When you lack
sufficient knowledge in a particular situation,
your good will will urge you to seek the
needed knowledge from those who have it.
However, in the ordinary situations of everyday living, you must rely on faith in yourself
and trust in God's assistance. Hope inclines
your spirit to draw its own conclusions from
your personal knowledge, experience, and
judgment.

9   Another common problem that needs the
supporting strength of supernatural hope, is
the problem of discouragement. If permitted
to thrive, discouragement becomes a de-
stroyer of faith. Discouragement is like a
mental cloud shutting out all inspiring vision
and weakening your positive attitudes. It
becomes a barrier to healthy ambition, a
cancer-like absorber of your vital energies, a

generator of insecurity and a breeder of anxiety. If left unchecked, discouragement can grow into the mind-crippling monster named "despair." Unfortunately, many people recognize discouragement only in its extreme manifestations. They do not realize that discouragement can hide behind many disguises, and work its evil in many indirect ways. Its victims may not even suspect that they are discouraged. They may go about their daily routine with their usual vague sense of frustration, failure, or even guilt. Though they may be constantly discontent, they fail to do anything about it. They feel no desire to get a true perspective of themselves, build new attitudes, seek new goals, or even make the best of a poor situation which must be tolerated at least for the present.

10 Due to the complexity of your human nature, it is almost impossible to avoid all discouragement in this earthly life. It is quite normal to feel some passing discouragement when you fail to achieve a cherished goal for which you worked so hard, or when you find yourself frustrated in some desire which is reasonable and good. This kind of discouragement presents no major obstacle to your self-possession. You can still think clearly,

judge wisely, and behave in accordance with your moral and religious principles. You need to beware of that discouragement which gradually wears down your enthusiasm for life and weakens your faith in yourself, in life, or even in God. The man of hope is well armed against this kind of discouragement.

11 Most people go about their daily activities with varying desires for a satisfactory achievement. However, human expectations can sometimes be quite unrealistic. People do not always face all the observable facts affecting their effort. True hope makes the spirit not only desirous of success, but also observant of circumstances which may block or limit one's success. In spite of your best intentions and sincerest efforts you will have your occasional failures, i.e., results that fail to equal your desires or expectations. Some people let their failures discourage them. A strong hope would urge them to try to understand why they failed, consider what they can do about it, and then proceed more wisely in their future efforts. This may be difficult when disappointment overwhelms the mind. Hope tends to put the "failure" into its proper perspective, by showing it for what it is, i.e., one individual part of a fulfillment

that promises much more than this "failure" took away. In other words, your hope keeps you looking forward to what fulfillment still lies ahead. It looks back only long enough to learn from the past. Where hope is weak, there is only useless lamenting and vain disappointment.

12   There is no sadder sight than that of a man of good will who does not know how to utilize and direct his good will. A number of people are open to good ideas, high ideals and noble causes. Yet, they live each day with a minimum of ambition, very little effort, and only mediocre achievement. If they could build up the virtue of hope within themselves, they might be inclined to re-assess their personal possibilities and actual limitations. With a realistic self-estimate and an adult desire to make the most of what they have, they could enrich their daily lives with achievements and satisfactions that now seem remote to them. Only those who are willing to see things as they really are, can effect such a change in their lives. True hope disposes the spirit to adopt such a willingness. It also prevents one from wanting more than can be in his circumstances, or desiring less than must be.

13   Beware of "stereotyping" yourself or others around you. Not everyone who seems lazy is truly lazy. Not every apparent "failure" is a true failure. People tend to judge others by appearances. In fact, some people misjudge themselves so much as to become discouraged or feel guilty about their poor achievement in daily life. They may be doing an injustice to themselves or others whom they judge blameworthy for a poor performance. Some people are really limited in their ability to perform. They lack the bodily energy or emotional strength to achieve any more than they do. Some, however, are victims of deep feelings of inadequacy, insecurity, and anxiety, which consume their physical energies through constant tension. Whether the problem is physiological or psychological, they find daily living much harder than their fellow-men do. They need more than encouragement. They may even need more than faith and hope. God usually expects man to apply natural remedies to natural problems. The biggest problem for some of these people is that they are ashamed to admit, perhaps even to themselves, that they have such a problem.

14   To some people the facts just presented

may seem like a lame excuse for sheer laziness, selfishness, or cowardice. Their thinking is done in such "black and white" that they reduce everything to a moral "good or bad" classification. This oversimplification of human nature is contrary to the facts. Every man lives in two worlds, namely, the world within him and the world around him. He is often unable to understand what he feels or why he feels it. This is why he needs the virtue of hope to help him redirect his faith when it is invaded by negative thinking. And yet, even with the positive thinking of his supernatural hope, there will be moments when his physical condition, mental disposition, and emotional tendencies will limit his ability to face life graciously. In spite of his best intentions, he will lack enthusiasm, be ultrasensitive or suspicious, feel bored with his routine, or display some form of hostility toward himself or others. When this occurs to you, you may be unable to do anything for yourself except express your hope and confidence in your own good will and God's fatherly understanding and blessing.

15   There is a group of people who seem to have few self-doubts, very little disappointment, and negligible discouragement in their

daily lives. They go through life with a state of mind which we call "presumption." These people take too much for granted, and always in their own favor. They expect more than they have objective reason to expect, and demand more than they have a right to demand. They act as though everyone has some obligation to respect their every wish and satisfy their every need, want, and desire. The presumptuous do not hesitate to take liberties at the expense of others. They seem to feel no concern for the needs of others, and no obligation to give others due consideration and respect. The presumptuous man is constantly reaching for more fulfillment and satisfaction than he is entitled to have by the facts and circumstances of his situation.

16 The motives which arouse each person to develop his particular personality are the needs, wants, and desires that stir within him. Each individual has his own pattern of intertwining drives, urges, emotions, fantasies, and thoughts. These move him toward the objects and goals in which he hopes to find fulfillment and satisfaction of his particular needs, wants, and desires. Some of your motives are conscious and some are unconscious. Some move you directly and some

indirectly. Thus, for instance, the presumptuous may behave as they do to prove their independence, assert their individuality, or protect themselves from possible threats from others. Whatever the immediate motivation, the deeper and primary motivation will always be the same. Every man needs to maintain and protect his sense of well-being from feelings of inadequacy, insecurity, and anxiety. Every disturbance of the sense of well-being will somehow involve these three basic disturbances. Thus, the victims of doubt, discouragement, and presumption all need a remedy which can offer some solution to the inadequacy-insecurity-anxiety problem. When natural remedies fail to provide a sufficient solution, you will have to turn to God for further assistance. Supernatural hope will dispose you to help yourself as far as you can, but it will also strengthen your reliance on God's personal cooperation with your efforts. A brief study of this remarkable virtue will deepen your understanding and intensify your appreciation of its divine power.

17   Hope contains three principal elements: The first element is a love and desire of the fulfillment for which your nature yearns. Natural hope is concerned only with the ful-

fillment obtainable in this earthly life. Supernatural hope also strives for earthly fulfillment, but it sees this fulfillment as only part
of the total fulfillment for which man was
created. Supernatural hope sees all earthly
fulfillment as necessary, but incomplete and
temporary. The man of supernatural hope is
convinced that his earthly fulfillment leads
him toward eternal life only if the earthly
fulfillment is achieved with the self-possession and self-management prescribed by
God's wise commandments. In its initial
stages, man's self-fulfillment is utterly self-
centered. With God's help and one's own
personal growth and experience, this fulfillment is gradually enlightened and directed
toward a broader love. Man comes to believe
in God's abiding presence in his spirit. He
finds himself reaching for a fulfillment that
lies beyond his earthly experience and is
above the level of his natural needs and wants.
In this supernatural union and cooperation
with God, man sees his own fulfillment and
God's glory as one and the same goal.

18   The second principal element of hope is
an abiding expectation of this supernatural,
all-satisfying, eternal fulfillment. Because
man cannot escape some measure of anxiety

in this life, anxiety about his possible failure to achieve his supernatural goal, he needs a counterbalance to this anxiety. He needs it to help him continue striving in spite of his insecurity and anxiety. Without this counterbalance, man could be overwhelmed by certain burdens, problems, and frustrations along his earthly path to God. He might surrender to his doubts, discouragement, or his urge to live presumptuously rather than realistically. Whatever his obstacles on earth, hope actually generates in him an expectation of performing satisfactorily and thereby gaining his desired fulfillment with God in heaven.

19   The third principal element of supernatural hope is man's own God-supported effort to make a sincere and wise use of the means which God places at his disposal. This element will be all the more determined and steadfast in proportion as one believes in the goodness, power, and love of God. This element of sincere determination to cooperate with God's inspirations and assistance, does not eliminate the defects and limitations of one's own personality. His natural past experience will still make itself felt through the recurrence of old undesirable habits, such as doubts and fears, passing discouragement,

and inclinations to presumption on the goodness of God and others. Hope works side by side with these natural defects and helps you direct them into healthy channels or control them in accordance with the requirements of each situation.

20 If you feel little or no enthusiasm about striving for a daily growth in faith and hope, look on this reluctance as your nature's resistance to change and its tendency to follow its established habits. You might also consider whether this reluctance contains some element of discouragement. A greater self-renewal seeks a greater self-possession, i.e., 1) greater freedom to think your own chosen thoughts, 2) greater freedom to make your own desired choices, 3) a greater control of your undesirable habits. On the other hand, you must be realistically idealistic. You need to accept the fact that you will never know all the answers to challenging situations. There will always be some occasions when you will have to be satisfied with whatever self-management you could achieve at the time. You will have to make an honest decision, and stick to it until you have reason to modify or change it. Supernatural hope will dispose you toward such a self-renewal.

It will also arouse in you a desire for the larger self-fulfillment presented to you by God's revelation, Christ's personal involvement in your life, and the constant sanctifying influence of the Holy Spirit.

21 You can never be too impressed by the following facts. An abiding perspective of these facts, can bring you greater balance and control amid the mental inadequacies and emotional disturbances which come to every man, each in his own particular manner and situations. Though you are enlightened by God's gifts of supernatural faith and hope, you are also limited by your natural needs, wants, and habits which operate not only on the conscious levels of your mind, but also those which function beneath and beyond your conscious awareness. Though you may deliberately choose to govern your behavior by God's supernatural revelation and daily inspirations, you will still have your natural, spontaneous, unwanted memories, imaginations, and emotions interfering with your deliberate efforts to accept God's truth, practice Christ's principles, and follow His example. You also need to understand how and why you fail to live up to these divine standards and ideals.

22   In proportion as you are willing and able to face facts and accept truth, you will look at yourself with a sincere desire to understand what needs, wants, and habits move you most often and most strongly. Beware of an unhealthy, unthinking, emotional tendency to blame yourself for all negative behavior or to turn your mind spontaneously from the entire subject. Look on this whole effort as a God-supported, methodical, "scientific" plan to grow into a more mature self-acceptance and a more adult self-management. With this matter-of-fact attitude, you will find yourself more disposed to reassess your present habits and motivations, rearrange your future intentions, and reorient your present self-renewal around this broader perspective of self-fulfillment.

23   The more you reflect on the preceding, the more you will appreciate how a solid supernatural hope disposes you to adopt an adult perspective in your reassessment and renewal of your daily life. A well-developed hope will make you willing to accept unexpected limitations in your efforts and unintended shortcomings in your achievement. It will also prepare you to tolerate inevitable disappointments and unforeseen frustrations.

With such an adult disposition, you will be disposed to assume a reasonable resignation when your best efforts fall short of their intended goal. The man of hope may be disappointed in the outcome of his ventures, but he is never discouraged by it, and he is certainly never disposed to surrender to despair, i.e., abandoning all hope of ever attaining success.

24 Some people live constantly under a mental and emotional shadow of doubt and fear. Though they never quite lose their faith, they do not enjoy its fortifying and consoling reassurance of God's love and His Son's work of redemption. Others, however, eventually lose their faith for lack of adult hope. They feel compelled to save their sanity from the destructive natural fears aroused by their mistaken image of God. Little do they realize that their idea of God is a false one. The God they turn away from, is not really the God who revealed Himself through His divine Son. They still live within the narrow limits of their childhood experiences, imagination, and emotions. In short, they never really grew up in their knowledge and personal acquaintance of the heavenly Father whom Jesus described in words and reflected by His personal example. A solid supernatural hope, developed patiently and trustingly through life, will slowly show them that God loves them more than they love themselves.

31

The Astonishing Power of Love

1 FAITH and hope are primary virtues. They are basic requirements for a successful and satisfying life on earth. Without faith and hope, life would be intolerable. Man would be overwhelmed by his doubts, fears, discouragement and despair. Everyone has his moments, when he is unsure about achieving some desired goal. At such times, you need to believe in yourself. Then again, there will be times when you are definitely inadequate to help yourself. On these occasions, you may have to depend on others. You will have to have some faith in their ability or willingness to help. So too with hope. Man has to fight against his self-doubts and discouragement by striving for his goals with an expectancy of achieving reasonably satisfactory results. Hope also helps him cope with inevitable disappointments and

unexpected failures. Hope disposes one to learn from his mistakes and work for further successes.

2 The more you believe in your ability to achieve, whether alone or with the help of others, so much the more confident will you feel in your daily routine. If you expect to succeed, you will face possible difficulties and actual obstacles more calmly than if you had a weak hope. Of course your faith and hope must be realistic. They ought to be based on all the facts and circumstances concerning the present situation, rather than on mere wishful thinking. An intelligent faith is based on knowledge, and a realistic hope takes into consideration whatever may influence one's efforts. Such a faith and hope provide a healthy counterbalance to one's feelings of inadequacy, insecurity and anxiety. In other words, these two virtues help you to: a) face life as is, b) improve what you can, and c) make the most of what cannot be improved.

3 There is a third basic virtue, necessary for a successful self-fulfillment in this earthly life. It is the virtue of charity. Like faith and hope, it enters into everything a person thinks, desires, says or does. Charity is another name for "supernatural" love. As

described in the second paragraph of chapter 29, charity differs from natural love in its 1) origin, 2) manner of operation, and 3) purpose. Charity is infused into man's spirit by God's direct supernatural union with him. This union moves man to seek his highest fulfillment and that of his fellow man with a deep regard for their common bond as children of God.

4   The truly charitable man has an awareness of God within himself and others. This awareness makes him identify himself with others and inclines him to care about their well-being as he does about his own. The charitable man sees God accepting this action as an act of supernatural love. Since God is "Supernatural Love Personified," He accepts man's charitable action as done to Him. This does not mean that the neighbor is not considered important in the charitable deed. On the contrary, he is respected and esteemed for his most excellent personal asset, namely his dignity as a child of God. This supernatural view of life inspires the man of charity to a high degree of concern for his neighbor's well-being. It is as genuine a concern as one may have for his own blood-brother.

5 With this understanding of charity, we are not surprised at Christ's answer, when asked what was the greatest commandment. His answer was derived from the Sacred Scriptures, which His questioners knew so well. "You must love the Lord your God with all your heart, with all your soul, and with all your mind." After stating that the second commandment resembled the first, He quoted again: "You must love your neighbor as yourself." Then with an authority that astonished his learned hearers, Jesus commented, "On these two commandments hang the whole Law and the Prophets also." (Matt. 22:34-40)

6 To those who may feel that this commandment is extremely difficult, if not impossible, we might suggest that they reflect on the discourse of Jesus at the Last Supper, as narrated in the thirteenth and fourteenth chapters of St. John's Gospel. A brief resume of those chapters might run somewhat as follows: Having stressed His union with His Father, Jesus proceeded to describe His union with His Disciples. He compared this union to the union of a vine and its branches, living one life together. He pointed out how a branch must die if separated from its source of life. He urged the Disciples to remain in His love, as friends remain loyal to one another. At this point, He foretold His sufferings for them, and followed this statement with a prediction of their future sufferings for His sake. He promised to stand by them through it all.

7 Jesus also promised to send them another "Comforter," the Holy Spirit. The Spirit was to dwell within them, enlighten their minds, and strengthen their efforts to spread the "Good News" of man's redemption and sanctification. Over and over, Jesus repeated His appeal for their personal love. He concluded His discourse with a long prayer to His Father for the success of His Disciples in their divine mission on earth. He prayed that they might become united with the Father and Him by a supernatural union of love and self-giving. The Disciples did not understand much of what Jesus said that night, but His central theme was clear. They were to prove their love by remaining faithful to Him amid the trials of life, as He Himself was to remain faithful to His Father in His own supreme proof of love.

8 As we reflect on the utter dedication of Jesus to His Father and His Disciples, we

may get some idea of the height, depth, breadth, and intensity of true love in its fullness. Jesus wanted a "one-ness" with His Disciples, somewhat like His "one-ness" with His Father. Though created man could never enter into the substantial, uncreated unity of the Holy Trinity, Jesus wanted His Disciples to be as fully joined to God as was humanly and divinely possible. Such is true love in its fullness. Love cannot get close enough, united enough, involved enough, or giving enough to the loved ones. Where love is full, to see a loved one is the same as seeing a part of oneself. There is an identity in true love, that makes the loving person ready to give and do as much for the loved one as for himself. In fact, as Jesus lived and died willingly for those He loved, so too does true love incline its subject to give of himself to those he loves. Of course, there can never be a perfect parallel between any created love and the uncreated love which belongs to God's very essence. That is why St. John wrote: " . . . God is love." (1 John 4:16) Any comparison between human love and divine love, must necessarily be analogical, i.e., so far from the full story as to leave a world of differences in spite of the comparison.

9 A number of people fail to understand the true nature of love. The child that shows concern about a sick parent, is generally considered to be expressing its love for the parent. Actually, he may be more concerned about the insecurity and anxiety which are disturbing his sense of well-being. The infatuations of youth are often viewed as an experience of "young love." More often than not, however, the individuals involved are each enjoying their own pleasant feelings, and living in the exhilarating daydreams that bring them so much inner contentment and joy. When their minds finally come back to reality, the romance wanes and fades away. Though true love may manifest some of the traits just described, it is basically different. Long after the rosy mist and rainbow of first impressions have left the horizon, the object of true love is still esteemed and desired in its reality.

10 In its depth, intensity, or duration, love is primarily an identification of the lover with the love-object, i.e., the person or thing loved. The love-object is perceived by the lover as wanted and needed for his own fulfillment and well-being. This reaching out for self-fulfillment, however, is only one element of true love. The lover also experiences a total identification with the love-object. He not only feels the love-object as a part of himself, but also feels himself as a part of the love-object. Whatever the loved one thinks, says, feels, or does, becomes important to the lover. He now finds his fulfillment in contributing to the well-being of the loved one. Whatever is seen as good for the love-object, is spontaneously desired and willingly done by the lover. In fact, in true and full love, the well-being and preservation of the love-object is felt by the lover as an extension of his own well-being and preservation. The central orientation, "I myself," that moves every man toward his own fulfillment, shifts to a new orientation, "we together," and this new self-center becomes the axis around which future fulfillment revolves. When this identification is complete, whatever the lover does for the love-object, is felt as done for himself as well. Such a degree of mutual love, makes two people live as one. The "selfishness" of each does not exclude, but includes the other.

11   Do not let the above description of love discourage you. True love in its fullness, is an ideal rarely achieved in this earthly life. Many people desire it, but must settle for less.

Every human being has his personal limitations, problems and conflicts. Each one has his particular needs and wants and his established habits by which he tries to fulfill his drives, wants and desires. Because of his need to maintain or restore his sense of well-being, man is limited in his ability to give of himself to others. Due to his constant drive to fulfillment and self-preservation, each individual is basically self-centered. As a result of this self-centeredness, every individual is somewhat separated from every other individual. The awareness of this separation, be it ever so deep, indirect, or indefinite, arouses some uneasiness in each individual person. He feels a need for friendship and good will, to restore his sense of well-being. Thus, you may see how man's self-centered nature is both the source of his craving for love and an obstacle to his self-giving.

12   In spite of the above obstacles, love is rooted in man's basic drive to self-fulfillment and self-preservation. The new-born infant is concerned only with his vital needs for food, comfort, and rest. As he becomes more aware of himself, his increasing needs, and the adults associated with these needs, he gradually feels an identity with these adults.

He begins to see them as "belonging" in his life, as he associates them with his sense of well-being. In proportion as he grows into further mental powers throughout the childhood stage of life, he experiences warm feelings toward these significant adults. His concern for their well-being is real but self-centered. He needs them safe and sound, if he is to have security and satisfaction. In other words, his love for them is a love of dependence.

13   Toward the end of childhood, the young individual undergoes a number of internal changes both in body and mind. He feels "different." He feels insecure. He is not sure how to go about being himself. He is body-conscious, self-conscious, and people-conscious. He sees himself as a budding adult, but is not quite sure how to manage his new powers. He is awkward and ill-at-ease with adults, even those who were previously close to him. If his training in sexual attitudes and behavior was too narrow, he may find sex a source of insecurity and anxiety. If sex was taught as a purely "religious" matter, he may fear it as a constant threat of "temptation" or "sin." In his desire to achieve "spotless purity," he may tend to worry

about how "deliberate or indeliberate" he was in thoughts, desires, or feelings related to sex. Many a person lost his original religious fervor through unrealistic self-doubts and torturing guilt-feelings about his natural sexual curiosity, attractions, or phantasies.

14   During this period of confusion and doubts, religious problems may arise. Religious faith may encounter difficulties that seem intellectual, but are often basically emotional. Religious hope may be shaken by frequent self-doubts or discouragements. Religious love may burn low amid feelings of inadequacy to live up to former ideals, insecurity with God, and anxiety concerning one's own eternal well-being. In sheer need to relieve this inner stress, the young adult may resort to skepticism or open disbelief. And yet, this revolt may not be primarily a religious matter. The teenager is also rebelling aginst the non-religious institutions and people whom he sees as "holding him down." Amid his confusing, conflicting emotions, he cannot appreciate the fact that they are working to keep him in line toward his necessary development and preparation for life. For the present he sees them only as representatives of "authority." Many or most

of these rebellious teenagers level off mentally and emotionally as they approach the end of their adolescent turmoil.

15   Even with the best of care and guidance, most teenagers cannot escape some measure of the mental and emotional turmoil just described. In their insecurity, they cling together with greater dependence than hitherto. They are easily influenced by "the group," since they have many needs and grievances in common. Understanding parents know how to let the teenager be himself within reasonable limits. They also know that certain duties are essential to the adolescent's future well-being. They try to blend freedom with justice in imposing the necessary duties of his age. They try to avoid treating him as a child. They also try to permit, or at least tolerate, his efforts to speak his mind in his own behalf. The adolescent dreams of his future as "something special." He also turns to thoughts of romantic love and yet at this particular time in life, most adolescents are unable to love realistically. They are simply too tied up with frequent strong needs and wants of their own to be concerned about the ordinary needs and wants of others. What they do for others is usually motivated by

their need for acceptance and approval by those whom they help, or by a need to feel important.

16   In proportion as parents are free of inner emotional problems of their own, they will be disposed to understand and help their growing children. They can show what true love really is by their understanding, and by patient efforts to communicate. Mature parents are mentally informed and emotionally balanced adults. They can show forth the love of God through their ready self-giving to their naturally insecure and awkward adolescent. At this stage in life, he needs time to develop his emerging spiritual powers of rational thought and moral responsibility. What appears to be "disrespect" in the adolescent, is often an attempt to break free of his inner feelings of inadequacy and insecurity. He is trying to feel "independent like an adult." He does not realize that adults also have their own feelings of inadequacy, insecurity, and anxiety about a number of things. If the teenager can be guided by true love through this stormy period of life, he will be better equipped to grow into a truly adult love of his own. In other words, he will gradually be disposed and able to: 1) identify

willingly with others, 2) give generously of himself, and 3) receive gratefully and graciously the sincere efforts of others to show their good will. He will gradually realize that love is far more than the physical intimacies and external gift-giving that often pass for proofs of true love.

17 The teenager who is fortunate enough to have such understanding parents, elders, and tutors, will experience within himself a growth of genuine love, a love springing from his sincere gratitude to those who gave willingly of themselves for his well-being. Though he may not yet comprehend the constant concern and self-sacrifice that true love requires of these parents and elders, he will have a fair idea of their sincere desire for his well-being throughout life. With such a positive disposition toward life, his spirit will experience less obstacles to its emerging powers of rational thinking and moral responsibility.

18 Towards the end of the teenage years, adolescence arrives at its full potential. The young adult begins to feel more self-reliant and self-respecting. His limitations in this development stem partly from his personal nature and partly from his negative habits of self-defense. Depending on his measure and

type of personality formation, the young adult now begins to appreciate his parents and elders more fully, as he faces more of life's responsibilities and requirements. He knows now, more than ever before, that life is an serious business and that his parents were busy all along the way, doing what they could to prepare their children for life's daily challenges, burdens and successes. In proportion as the newly formed adult is free of any unusual personality defect, he is now able to identify willingly and understandingly with other adults. He is disposed to give of himself, and to find his own satisfaction and contentment in contributing to the satisfaction and contentment of others. He has grown into the age of true love, i.e., the love of benevolence or friendship. With time, experience, and wisdom learned from his own limitations and mistakes, and enriched by God's continued blessings and inspirations, his true love will grow in depth, height, breadth, and intensity. He will be capable of a greater self-possession, i.e., living more realistically close to his own feelings, thoughts, desires, and efforts. He will also be able to live in closer friendship with God and his fellow men.

19 It is astonishing how difficult it is to

convince some people that they are capable
of enlarging their present measure of true
love. Some are even skeptical of the very
idea of "love." Their present ability to love
is quite limited by their deep feelings of
personal inadequacy to deal successfully with
many situations in everyday life. Just as they
are unsure of themselves in other areas of
life, so too are they unsure of their ability to
exercise love for others or to receive love
graciously from others. Some are ill at ease
with people because they are not sure that
they can hold the good will of others for any
length of time. Their own good will is easily
shaken by the unpredictable moods of others.
They dread possible rejection, whether
through disagreement in ideas or through
some other form of disapproval. The root
problem of these insecure people, is that they
do not love themselves realistically. Even
though they are constantly demanding that
things go their way, they make this demand
in order to avoid disturbing self-doubts,
self-blame, or some other unhealthy form of
self-discontent.

20   True love is possible only to people who
have a balanced self-love, i.e., 1) due concern
for their own well-being, 2) a realistic belief

in their personal worth as an individual, and 3) a warranted respect for their own tastes, preferences, judgment and opinions. People who love themselves in this manner, are at ease enough to be themselves without showing undue disregard for others. They do not feel obliged to agree unwillingly with others, nor do they feel compelled to convince those who disagree with them. They are considerate of other people's legitimate feelings and sincere convictions. They are interested enough in truth to listen to the views of others, and honest enough to hold on to their own view when convinced of it. They are not unduly afraid of what others may say or think because they know that every man is subjective in many things. Finally, the man who loves himself with a balanced self-concern, knows that God sees his honest disposition of good will, whatever his limitations or failures. Being able to believe in himself, he is also able to believe in God's understanding, and is disposed to live in peace and friendship with others.

21 Do not think that such a balanced self-love is impossible to you. It might have been, had not God given you a strong, supernatural motive for believing in your supernatural

worth and dignity. True, your natural emotional habits may diminish your faith in yourself or weaken your confidence in your self-renewal. On the other hand, in the life of Jesus we have visible proof that such a self-renewal is not only possible, but definitely achievable. It may not be as easy as you might like, but then neither is it impossible. You have the assurance of Jesus Himself that He will stand by you in your effort. Just as He never mentioned the utter panic and desertion of His Disciples after His resurrection, neither will He think less of you for an imperfect performance or recurring failures. He knows only too well that it requires a stronger love to keep trying in the face of repeated failures, than to keep trying amid signs of progress, be it ever so slow and imperfect. Only the quitter has stopped loving.

22 Jesus provided us with the kind of motive we need as He revealed His plan of redemption to His Disciples. He was speaking not only for them, but also for every man who would accept His "Good News" down through the centuries. For the moment, they felt close to Him, but their feeling of "belonging" was soon to be shaken and shattered. Though they were now at peace in the light of His presence

and the Warmth of His love, they would shortly be frightened, confused, weak, alone, and utterly discouraged. Knowing all this, Jesus was telling them the secret of their future success. They were to remain ever joined to Him in a strong bond of love. He put it this way: "I shall ask the Father and He will give you another Advocate to be with you forever, the Spirit of truth whom the world can never receive, since it neither sees nor knows him. But you know him, because he is with you, he is in you. I will not leave you orphans: I will come back to you. In a short time the world will no longer see me; but you will see me, because I live and you will live. On that day you will understand that I am in my Father and you in me and I in you." (John 14:16-21)

23   St. Paul learned this lesson of Christian identification at the very outset of his conversion. The risen Christ introduced Himself to Paul with the words: "I am Jesus, and you are persecuting me." (Acts 9:5) In his later writings, Paul stressed this identification in Christ many times. He reminded his converts of their "one-ness" in Christ. He reminded them of their variety of activities in the development of the body of Christ, i.e ,

the Church. He pointed out how each man's personal gifts contributed to the joint effort in Christ's cause. He stressed how they needed one another and warned them against envy and interpersonal rivalry, since they were all one in Christ. (1. Cor. 12:1-31)

24 This is the motivation that can inspire you to respect yourself, and to be reasonably concerned about others. With such a positive attitude toward yourself, you will be more spontaneous in manifesting good will toward others. The more aware you become of Jesus in yourself and in others, so much the more will you be disposed to give of yourself to those who are in need of some encouragement or assistance. It may not be more than a smile, a kind word, an understanding ear, a bit of patience, a generous overlooking of people's shortcomings, but each of these is an act of love. They are acts of concern and consideration for the well-being of others. Most of these acts require little time and not too much exertion, but they are no less precious to the receiver and to Jesus. As far as He is concerned, you did it to Him, and He will say so in the presence of all mankind at the last judgment. (Matt. 25:31-41)

25 Paul never tired of urging his fellow

Christians to remain aware of their "oneness" in Christ's love. He called charity the "bond of perfection." Nothing completes a person as much as love does. Whatever else may be lacking, the good natured person, the understanding and accepting person, the generous person, the interested person, the helpful person—in short, the loving person inspires some degree of love in those around him. When love is kindled in the spirit by one's personal contact with Christ, it burns bright and strong on a higher level of self-giving. The Christian lover wishes everyone the very best of everything he needs. It is not only a true love, but it is a wise love as well. It is a love that proceeds from the revealed truth of God, the personal example of Christ, and the guidance and strengthening of the Holy Spirit within every man of good will. True love seeks the best fulfillment and the highest well-being of the loved ones.

26   In the following passage, St. Paul draws a verbal picture of the truly loving Christian: "You are God's chosen race, His saints; He loves you and you should be clothed in sincere compassion, in kindness and humility, gentleness and patience. Bear with one another; forgive each other as soon as a quarrel begins.

The Lord has forgiven you; now you do the same. Over all these clothes, to keep them together and complete them, put on love. And may the peace of Christ reign in your hearts, because it is for this that you were called together as parts of one body. Always be thankful . . . With gratitude in your hearts, sing psalms and hymns and inspired songs to God and never say or do anything except in the name of the Lord Jesus, giving thanks to God the Father through Him. (Col. 3:12-17)

27 Paul simply could not say enough about the supreme quality of love. He wrote to the Corinthian Christians: "If I have all the eloquence of men or of angels, but speak without love, I am simply a gong booming or a cymbal clashing. If I have the gift of prophecy, understanding all the mysteries there are, and knowing everything, and if I have faith in all its fullness, to move mountains, but without love, then I am nothing at all. If I give away all that I possess, piece by piece, and if I even let them take my body to burn it, but am without love, it will do me no good whatever. (1. Cor. 13:1-3)

28 Paul then goes on to show why the virtue of charity is the mother of every other virtue: "Love is always patient and kind; it is never

jealous; love is never boastful or conceited; it is never rude or selfish; it does not take offense, and is not resentful. Love takes no pleasure in other people's sins, but delights in the truth; it is always ready to excuse, to trust, to hope, and to endure whatever comes. Love does not come to an end . . . In short, there are three things that last; faith, hope, and love, and the greatest of these is love." (1. Cor. 13:4-13)

29 Do not let this ideal picture discourage you. It was meant to show you that man never reaches a stage in life where he may no longer hope for some further growth in spirit. If you are convinced of this and accept it as a normal condition of earthly living, you will never be bored, or discouraged, or disgusted, or straining for results. Love is a lifetime virtue. For this reason, love never pushes anyone beyond his endurance, nor does it demand more than he can give at the moment. Jesus praised the widow who donated her last cent to the temple. On the other hand, He would not have thought less of her, had she kept it to buy a piece of bread for herself or her children. God accepts our good will as we are able to express it at the time. Until you can see this "sweet reasonableness" of God being reflected in the attitudes and example of Jesus, you will always be in danger of mistaking your own unreasonable emotional standards for the will of God or the voice of conscience. If this happens, you will turn away from Christ or follow Him at a distance. You will also find yourself hemmed in by your natural inadequacy, insecurity, and anxiety with all the unhealthy mental and emotional consequences which they bring with them. Jesus would rather have us hold on to Him because we need Him, than leave Him because of our confusing doubts and misleading discouragements. He loves us as we are, and He would have us love ourselves the same way. Do this and you shall live a fuller and more satisfying life both here and hereafter.